The Structure of Plato's Philosophy

The Structure of Plato's Philosophy

Jerry S. Clegg

Lewisburg
Bucknell University Press
London: Associated University Presses

Associated University Presses, Inc.
Cranbury, New Jersey 08512

Associated University Presses
Magdalen House
136–148 Tooley Street
London SE1 2TT, England

Library of Congress Cataloging in Publication Data

Clegg, Jerry S
The structure of Plato's philosophy.

Bibliography: p.
Includes index.
1. Plato. I. Title.
B395.C58 184 75-31467
ISBN 0-8387-1878-7

PRINTED IN THE UNITED STATES OF AMERICA

For Cardie and Marion

Contents

Preface

There are two sorts of reasons people have had for writing books about Plato. Some authors have been partisans of a philosophical cause, trying to expose or to bolster what they have seen as the pernicious or the wholesome in Plato's work. In contrast, others have had the more restrained ambition of simply trying to convey their ideas on how Plato is best to be understood. To my mind the most provocative and absorbing books about Plato have been written in a partisan spirit. It is therefore with some regret that I acknowledge my own ambitions to be of the more restrained sort. I merely want to convey what I hope is a unifying and explanatory account of basic Platonic doctrines. This is not because I have no opinions on the merit of those doctrines. I do. I think many of them are false, and I would find many more of them repugnant if forced to live by them. Nonetheless, for a pair of reasons, I do not choose to dwell on these matters. The range of issues I want to address is wide enough to make it impractical to offer all the arguments against Plato that would have to be offered to give any interest to my demurs. I am also enough of a partisan of Plato the man, if not of his doctrines, that I find it easy to appreciate with an almost aesthetic equanimity his practice of accepting the ramifications of his arguments no matter how high in disquiet or low in plausibility they are. By conviction, then, I cannot be a partisan apologist for Plato, yet I am neither in a position nor of a mind to quarrel with him. Accordingly, my ambitions are limited to interpreting certain facets of his work, and I would caution my reader that although the absence of critique in this book may be taken as a symptom of a friendly interest in Plato, it should not be mistaken for the presence of any belief in the truth of his doctrines.

My ambitions, limited as they are, are still fairly strenuous. I would like to accomplish three things. First of all, I want to identify Plato's position on a number of central topics. Deciding what a major philosopher actually maintained is often far from easy, but it is particularly hard to do in Plato's case. His arguments and language can be as opaque as any other writer's, and his methods and style of exposition offer problems of their own. Characters in his dialogues who seem to serve as his spokesmen sometimes appear to contradict each other; at times, too, a single spokesman will argue against a tenet in one dialogue that seems obviously crucial to his stand in another. Hints of burlesque and satire also serve to mask Plato's intent. The chief problem, however, is psychological. Plato is in many ways an enormously attractive and intelligent writer who, nonetheless, appears to argue for some very strange, disquieting positions. In those cases there is a temptation, difficult to master, to rescue him from his own prose and to give him asylum in one's own faith or, failing that, in a view that one can regard as reasonably plausible, wise, or generous. To do anything less has seemed to many of his commentators—even those with no partisan cause to defend—to be irresponsible. His texts, they have often felt, simply cannot be taken at face value. As a result, there is no firm consensus on what Plato's views are regarding topics that range from metaphysics to politics. Indeed, there is a working consensus that he had no set views on a number of central issues. Many modern scholars, for example, hold that in spite of all his discussions Plato had no theory of art or of politics. It is frequently argued, too, that he had no single doctrine on the nature of the soul and that he couldn't, or at least didn't, make up his mind about how his Forms were to be described. For my part, I think that there is more consistency and clarity in Plato than most of his interpreters have been willing to admit. I shall try to make good on that judgment by moving to identify the stands he takes. In several crucial cases I will do that by trying to show why his ostensive doctrines should be taken at face value.

My second ambition is to map onto each other the doctrines I take to be those Plato is committed to. I want to show the structural unity of his thought, and I want to do that not just because it is a way of lending credence to my views on what his stands are, but also because I think a large part of the interest Plato must hold for anyone lies in the way he allows his argument to proceed from one seemingly unrelated topic to another. Some of his epistemological claims, for example, appear to me to dictate certain biological conclusions that deeply affect, in turn, his psychology, his critique of the fine arts, and his political views. An important number of my theses concern thematic links of this kind between Plato's doctrinal stands.

Last of all, I want to contribute in some progressive way to an understanding of Plato. If I am successful in my other ambitions I can scarcely fail in this one; still, it needs to be mentioned in its own right, for it sets a limited scope to this book in a way my other ambitions do not. I have mentioned the lack of agreement among authorities about Plato. That lack of agreement, although extensive, is by no means all encompassing. Most of the particular arguments used by Plato have been analyzed clearly and well by others in commentaries that are readily available to anyone interested in following the conversations his dialogues purport to record. For this reason it would be an idle enterprise from my point of view to write about the whole of Plato's work, and I have no intention of doing so. I do want to present a fairly complete account of his major doctrines, but not on a dialogue-by-dialogue basis, which would only duplicate much of what others have already done. Rather, I want to concentrate on the outstanding, unresolved issues in Platonic scholarship. Thus, after an initial discussion of his philosophical motivations, I will move to consider what most of Plato's interpreters have viewed as key questions in his metaphysics, his theory of knowledge, his psychology, his theory of art, and his politics. This is not an exhaustive range of topics. Still, it is not a narrow one either; and I hope the result of my efforts will be a unifying and explanatory account of essential doctrines in Plato's work that is broad enough in its scope, yet focused enough on hard, unresolved issues, to be of interest to everyone with an interest in Plato.

J.S.C.

Trial Lake, Utah

Acknowledgments

I would like to express my gratitude to Mills College for a grant to cover the costs of preparation of the manuscript; to my wife for her spirited help in detecting errors; and to Mrs. Mathilde E. Finch for her expert assistance in editing the manuscript.

The Structure of Plato's Philosophy

Introduction: Plato's Ambitions

Plato's dialogues reflect as broad a range of interests as almost any author has ever pursued. There is scarcely any field of inquiry he did not contribute to, if only by way of intelligent comment. His contributions, too, were serious enough to have had their impact. No one's knowledge of the history of subjects as divergent as theology and linguistics, or political science and aesthetics, or mathematics and psychology, could be reasonably complete without an awareness of Plato's views and their almost perennial reappearance in the work of others. His dialogues have also been—with only the exception of the Bible—the richest referent of literary and philosophical allusions in our traditions. They are, without question, one of the great source books of our culture.

The breadth of Plato's interests and the near universality of the impact of his doctrines stand in extraordinary contrast to the narrowness and the virtual uniqueness of his core ambitions. In what he wrote about all the subjects he took up there are certain principles of argument that point to a relentless drive on his part to satisfy but two basic, joined, and eager desires. Those desires have only occasionally been shared by the myriad of writers who have borrowed from him or have been stimulated by his work, for he wrote in an effort to resolve a pair of intellectual problems that were, in their intertwined relations, largely peculiar to his age. Certainly they are problems that few have taken as seriously as he did. Certainly, too, they are problems that only a handful have seen as intimately related as he saw them. More certainly yet, they are problems that virtually no one has tried to resolve with the help of the strategies he devised. They remain, nonetheless, problems that define his philosophy. By way of an introduction to the themes and structure of this book I want to identify but a pair of powerfully simple Platonic concerns.

Plato was a dualist. And he was a dualist in two senses. He drew a distinction between a reality that he felt could be known and a realm of appearance that he felt could not be known. He also drew a distinction between two kinds of appearance. One kind, rarer than the other, he described as controlled by a rational principle of action and as being as just and as intelligibly akin to reality as is possible. Another kind he described as controlled by an irrational principle and as being unjust and less like reality than it should be. What Plato called reality served in his mind as some kind of moral as well as intellectual standard. It ought, he felt, to guide our conduct. It also ought to be subject of our most serious inquiries and the model for our art, for it alone can be fully understood. Unfortunately, in Plato's view, we seldom model our conduct on reality, and only occasionally do we treat it as the subject of our arts and sciences. The reason we neglect it so is that it is without empirical qualities. The world we live in belongs entirely to the realm of appearance; it is natural that most of us should be unaware of even the existence of a reality we never see or touch or hear. It is equally natural that we should look to aspects of our own world for guidance or enlightenment when troubled or puzzled. It takes a thoughtful person—one with a rare philosophical disposition—to answer questions about what is just and what is true by examining, with the aid of thought alone, the unsensed structure of reality.

It is easy to see that Plato was in some measure a scientific and moral skeptic. Nothing about the world was, in his eyes, fully intelligible or fully just. It is easy to see, too, that his dualisms were devised as ways of limiting the force of his skepticism. If nothing in the world of appearance is a full standard of truth or rectitude, then there is at least another, more real world where those standards can be found. Once found, they can be used by reasonable men to combat the irrationalities of life and to make the world more just as well as more intelligible than, for the most part, it now is. An improved appearance is possible. We do not have to accept what is or has been as a test of what should be. Plato's dialogues are the work of a man trying to extricate himself from his own skepticism. His discussions, arguments, rhetorical speeches, and myths are a kind of intellectual planetary system dominated by a solar core of disquieting conviction. He simply accepted as true certain skeptical motifs that call into doubt both science and culture and that lie at the center of his work. More than anything else, however, he wished to avoid the nihilistic implications others had drawn from those same motifs. The tension between conviction and desire results in an elaborate doctrinal system that is far removed from traditional skepticism, but that still revolves in an orderly way around traditionally skeptical stands.

In describing Plato in these dualistic terms I am, of course, describing Plato himself as both a participant in and a critic of the intellectual temper of his times. He was born in Athens between, authorities say, 429 and 427 B.C. In his youth he lived through the early years of the Peloponnesian war. Later he experienced the defeat of Athens by Sparta. In his adolescence he must have heard firsthand the plottings of his aristocratic relations who helped overthrow Athenian democracy. He must, too, have been thoroughly familiar with the postwar moral and political cynicism that justified intrigue and arbitrary rule of the weak by the strong. One may presume that his distaste for the cynicism of his day was a reason for his decision not to embark on a political career, which would have been open to him, but instead to attach himself as a disciple to the enigmatic Socrates—a man of great personal probity and eloquence whose ironic critiques of Athenian life ended only with his execution in 399 by the officials of a restored democratic regime. Upon the death of Socrates, Plato is said to have left Athens for more than a decade. Upon his return he founded the Academy and spent the rest of his career as a teacher and administrator of what was to become the world's most famous institution of higher learning. The span of Plato's mature life marked the end of a political age. Shortly after his death in 348 B.C. the independent city-state was to be no more. The Macedonian and then the Roman empires soon absorbed the whole of Greece. In the meantime, however, Plato lived out his life in the kind of intense intellectual atmosphere that has frequently characterized the small, cosmopolitan, and independent city-state. He became a defender of the style of life he knew, and he engaged with very considerable vigor in the philosophical debating that many authorities attest to as one of the more pronounced and remarkable features of Athenian life. For more than forty years he was the very epitome of the urban intellectual devoted to inquiry in all its forms. If there is anything that distinguished him from the colleagues and compatriots he worked with, argued with, sometimes satirized, and tried to learn from, it was not that he had a taste they lacked for thought and learning, but rather it was the self-consciousness with which he tried to justify what he, and they, were; for there is a sense in which his entire philosophy is an exercise in self-justification. The reason he tried to justify himself is, of course, his feeling that a justification was required, and he felt that way because in certain fundamental respects he harbored doubts about the possibility of knowledge and the wisdom of leading a urban existence. It was his scientific and moral skepticism that drove him to a defense of the inquisitive, civilized life he led and loved. The structure of his philosophy is a function of the argumentative defense he devised.

One may surmise that Plato's skepticism is in part the result of his observing the ignorance and folly of men, for his dialogues have a full measure of sardonic reflections on human frailty. Primarily, however, his skepticism has its source in the purely philosophical work of his contemporaries and immediate predecessors. He was well acquainted with the disturbing views of such men as Parmenides, his pupil Zeno, and the sophists Antiphon and Callicles. Their arguments led to nihilistic conclusions he was anxious to avoid on the possibility of empirical science, on the propriety of living in an urban, civilized setting, and on the intelligibility of ordinary moral judgments. Yet, Plato obviously felt the power of their arguments, for crucial elements in them compose the nucleus of his own position. Just as obviously, however, he was not himself a nihilist. As a supplement to my initial description he could, then, be described as man who took to heart the most provocative intellectual issues of his age, trying to balance the rival claims within them by paying to the skeptical nihilist most of his due but without accepting from him the whole of his lesson.

The relation of Plato to his skeptical contemporaries and predecessors is complex. Virtually all the points I wish to make about his work, however, are related to a single pair of skeptical motifs that he takes, in effect, for granted. Both motifs involve invidious analyses of contrasting terms. The first analysis contrasts things at rest with those in motion, only to find the former intelligible and real, the latter unintelligible and illusory. The second analysis contrasts convention or art (*nomos*) with nature (*physis*), only to scorn the former as decadent or perverse and to revere the latter as in some way the hallmark of virtue and justice. Plato accepts the two associations in these analyses of reality with rest and nature with justice. These are associations that, taken together, form what I have already described as the disquieting, skeptical core of his system to which almost everything else reacts.

The invidious contrast between intelligible, real rest and unintelligible, illusory motion had its origin in the famous paradoxes of the philosopher Parmenides and his pupil Zeno. Zeno's book, which he called *Wranglings* and which Plato must have known, appears to have equated motion with division on the ground that there is no significant difference between proportionately cutting up a plank into parts and walking along it. Each footfall, Zeno seems to have reasoned, can be viewed as a point of potential division. He then pointed out that if space is a continuum, division could theoretically proceed forever, but that if it is discrete—and so not a continuum—division must necessarily be finite. In either case, he argued, we can make no sense out of division or, by extension, motion of any kind.

A noncontinuous space composed of indivisible units of volume would give us no way of coherently measuring distance or time. We would have no way, for example, of reconciling the relative speed of two teams of runners moving in single file and in opposite directions past each other with their different, absolute speeds as measured against a stationary set of markers placed on the discrete dividing lines of space. The relative speed of a runner might be "two runners" a minute; his absolute speed might be "one marker" a minute. But if space is discrete we have no way of saying where he was in terms of the stationary markers when, measured against members of the oppositely moving team, he had traveled the equivalent of one marker. We would be tempted to say that he was halfway between two markers, but that assumes space is forever divisible and so conflicts with the hypothesis under scrutiny. Versions of Zeno's argument have long been taken as demonstrating that both space and time cannot be discrete.

A continuous space, on the other hand, would give us, in Zeno's view, no prospect of ever completing even the shortest journey, for by definition we cannot finish the task of proportionately dividing a length into an infinite set of points. No runner can ever cross the goal line he draws near. No arrow can ever reach its target. But if we cannot finish a journey, we cannot start one either, since any interval can be viewed as a completed journey. Arrows cannot even leave their bows. Runners cannot even get off their starting lines. Zeno's conclusion, like Parmenides', was that motion—although attested to by the eye—is unintelligible, even unreal, and that all words such as *time* and *change*, which imply the opposite, are senseless. Only the eternal and the immobile are intelligible, real, and capable of being significantly described. Thus in his book *On Nature*, Parmenides carefully distinguished between an initial "truthful" talk of a reality at rest and a subsequent set of "lying" words about the moving, thoroughly illusory objects of sensory experience.

It is obvious that there is much in the position of Parmenides that Plato accepted. He did not try to break Zeno's arguments. Neither did he—as the philosophers Protagoras and Gorgias apparently did—challenge Parmenides and Zeno on the ground that sense experience is the only criterion of what is coherent and that, therefore, the reasoned indictment of the testimony of the senses on the reality of motion must be unsound. He agreed that reason, not sensation, has to be the arbiter of what is and is not significant and true. He agreed, too, that there is something about motion that is conceptually incoherent. In developing his theory of the Forms, for example, he held that the fully intelligible can only be eternal and immobile (*Phaedrus* 247 C). He also held that what isn't fully intelligible cannot be either fully real or fully describable. Changeable things can only be appearances, and they cannot be known or spoken of in truth. The best we can manage by way of thought or speech about moving, empirical matters is to construct a story, or *mythos*, which has to be sharply distinguished from a true account, or *logos*. In these ways Plato accepted the extreme tenets of a position that fosters, even seems to demand, skeptical conclusions on the possibility of empirical science. If motion is unintelligible, surely moving things cannot be explained, and most of human inquiry is a wasted effort.

The second invidious contrast I have mentioned as central to Plato's system is that between an indictable artifice (*nomos*) and a commendable nature (*physis*). This contrast was used by several sophists of Plato's day. It was used as the basis of a critique of the social, political, legal, and moral codes of Greek society, and it threatened in its extreme usage to indict the whole urban character of city-state civilization. The sophist Antiphon, for example, contrasted in the lifetime of Socrates the laws of nature to the conventional rules of man, arguing that for the most part things deemed just by convention are hostile to nature and chains upon it. It is natural, his point was, to seek our self-interest, and so unnatural to do our duties by others. Since what is natural is assumed to be the highest possible principle of morality, Antiphon's argument amounts to the judgment that a morality enforced by custom and law is a morality we are under no genuine obligation to obey. The natural law that enjoins us to seek our self-interest dictates that we abide by the conventional laws of the state only when, as in the presence of witnesses, it is obviously in our interest to obey them. Plato ascribes a view similar to Antiphon's to the sophist Callicles (*Gorgias* 482 E) and to other, unnamed spokesmen of a materialist school of thought that professed scorn for everything conventional and artificial (*Laws* 890 A). It is a view that invites the conclusion that ordinary moral judgments can be based only on appeals to statutes and customs and are therefore groundless, lacking both force and sense. It also invites the conclusion that a life lived totally in accord with nature, apart from the restraining influence of convention, would be the perfectly just life. Since such a life is difficult, if not impossible, to lead in the confines of an urban state, the very form of life ancient civilization took becomes suspect if the natural is adopted in Antiphon's manner as the hallmark of the just. A suspicion of that kind would seem to have been rife in Plato's day. His contemporary Antisthenes criticized Athenian society on the ground that it was unnatural, and Diogenes later presented the barrel in which he chose to live, his nakedness, and his independence as a reproach to his fellow Corinthians, clothed and housed as they were in artifice and leading lives governed by superficial, unnatural convention. A similar indictment of urban life on the ground of its unnaturalness appears in the Cyrenaic and Cynic schools, whose members sought to live in a state of nature either by removing themselves to the wilds of North Africa—as did the followers of Aristippus, another of Plato's contemporaries—or by rejecting conventional codes of etiquette in favor of imitating the uncouth behavior of animals—as did the Cynics, who became notorious for their effort to live like dogs.

As in the case of Parmenides' indictment of empirical science, it is obvious that there is much in this position, too, that Plato accepted. He did not—again as Protagoras and others apparently did—challenge those of Antiphon's persuasion by contrasting the benefits of civilization to the dangers and discomforts of a raw state of nature, thereby trying to establish the superiority of the artificial over the natural. Plato clearly used the word *nature* in an honorific sense, leaving to *convention* a derogatory import. The natural, he agreed, is always to be prefered to the artificial. He also agreed that the laws, customs, and institutions of the Greek city-state were matters of convention, not nature (*Laws* 889 D - 892 A). He accepted, then, the fundamentals of a position that seems both to undermine ordinary moral principle and to leave unsanctioned the urban form of life of classical culture.

Yet, in accepting these two invidious analyses of motion and convention, Plato never went so far as to accept the scientific and moral skepticism they so clearly fostered in his compatriots. Indeed, the major philosophical ambition of his life was to find some way of justifying empirical science, conventional morality, and the urban character of civilization. The moving cosmos may not be fully intelligible, but it is not, he insisted, the mere incoherent illusion that Parmenides judged it to be. We can at least partially explain and understand it. So also, the laws and institutions of a society may be matters of mere convention, not nature, but we still have good reason for abiding by them and accepting as our proper home the city-state.

To reach these conclusions Plato engineered two escapes from his skeptical convictions. They differ in kind, but they do resemble each other in key respects. They also meet to form the basis of his metaphysics and his cosmology. They thus provide the connecting routes between his theories of knowledge and science and his theories of culture and art. A full survey of the escape routes Plato devised will not be complete until this book is finished. A preliminary sketch of them can be of some use, however, by way of illuminating the format of the chapters to follow and clarifying yet more precisely the basic ambitions that drove Plato to write.

Plato indirectly defends the epistemological priority of thought over sensation by trying to escape the full indictment of empirical science by Parmenides and Zeno through a limitation on the force of their contrast between illusory motion and real rest. The goal of all moving things, he points out, is to be at rest. Thus the terminal of a completed action and the goal of the action coincide. If, for some reason, rest is denied to a moving thing, its goal is still to be at rest. The heavens move continuously, for example, but their regular motion is part of an effort to be as nearly like an indivisible realm of rest as they possibly can. Indeed, an element in the change characteristic of all the objects of sensory experience is a struggle to be like a changeless, fully intelligible, knowable reality (*Phaedo* 75 A). Their struggle allows them to "partake of" or "participate in" the intelligible nature of an eternal, immobile order. Their participation then gives to them a degree of coherence and makes them at least partially understandable. Empirical science may never provide us with exact knowledge of anything, but because its changeable objects resemble those we can know, it can provide us with "true opinions," and its practice is not, therefore, an idle pursuit. The crucial point in this preliminary sketch of Plato's position is that he refuses to treat *motion* and *rest* as the contraries Parmenides and Zeno, plausibly enough, took them to be. His analyses elevate the supposedly unintelligible motion into a defective version of intelligible rest. The moving, empirical cosmos is ontologically related to an immobile, intelligible realm as appearance, not illusion, is related to reality. The element of motion in the cosmos is itself related to rest as the apparent is related to the real. That relation is not one of opposition and contradiction; it is a relation of resemblance. We can, Plato's point is, give some degree of coherence to the concepts *motion, time*, and *change* by treating what we call these things as a kind of defective version, or blurred image, of the state of rest that is only sometimes the attained terminal, but always the ultimate goal, of moving things. Change, motion, and time itself are images of an abiding, static eternity (*Timaeus* 37 C-E). The whole of Plato's doctrine may not be easy to understand, but the point it tries to establish is clear: time, as an image, is an imperfect version, not the opposite, of the eternity it somehow pictures. The motive behind Plato's doctrine is also clear. If there is no full contradiction between the imprecise testimony of the senses and the more precise testimony of thought, then we have no reason to indict the latter as standing refuted by the former. We must, of course, realize that thought and sensation will never agree completely and that we must, accordingly, pronounce the world of sensory experience partially incoherent.

Plato tries to escape the indictment by Antiphon and Callicles of conventional morality and urban life with the help of a maneuver that is similar in effect, but different in execution from his handling of the terms *motion* and *rest*. He undermines the use of the invidious contrast between *art* and *nature*. He does not, however, claim that the indicted term in this contrast, *art*, is a defective version of the unindicted term, *nature*. Rather, he argues that what we are accustomed to call nature is really a form of art. He downgrades, so to speak, the revered instead of elevating the scorned to limit the force of the troublesome contrast. As a further difference, he makes no use of an ontological distinction between appearance and reality to effect his end. Instead, he relies on what I will call a teleological distinction between agencies that is internal to the realm of appearance itself. What deserves to be called culture is, for Plato, rational, human art; what we call nature is really irrational, divine art (*Sophist* 265 E). If the equation of nature with divine art can be maintained, then the position of all those who would attack the artificial and the conventional in the name of the natural is overthrown. They cannot point to a code of conduct or way of life that is any less artificial than that to be found in the milieu of the city-state. Selfishness, nakedness, and the untilled wastes of the world belong just as much to the realm of convention (*nomos*) as duty, clothes, and city pavement. Of course one might argue that divine conventions are to be preferred to human conventions, but Plato offers considerations that purport to show how unreasonable such an argument would be. Given the failure of the normal contrast between art and nature, his position is that we have good reason to prefer our own, human art to that which is, in being divine, alien to us.

Even so, one might still argue that a truly natural estate apart from all culture, human or divine, would be the ideal setting for us; and with that sentiment Plato seems to agree. The true home of the human soul is in a natural realm apart from the artifice of the world. Given our presence in the world, however, we must make do with the best we can manage, and that is to live within the moral and political confines of the city-state. Just as we have to accept something less than a full understanding of the world in our empirical inquiries, so we have to accept something less than a full justification of our cultural estate in our political deliberations. The intelligible maintains a priority over the empirical, and the natural remains superior to the artificial. Yet both empirical science and culture are defended.

The two maneuvers Plato uses to justify science and culture involve, it is clear, the partial undermining of the invidious contrasts that bother him. What his underminings amount to is also clear. He simply replaces the two contrasts with distinctions that imply some form of similarity or identity between the things distinguished. As *motion* is a disorderly, apparent version of *rest*, so *nature* is a divine form of *art*. These distinctions mesh. The moving cosmos, which is the realm of appearance in Plato's ontological distinction, is primarily the nature that is redefined as divine art in what I have called his teleological distinction. Human art, of course, is a minor part of the cosmos as well. Thus one must conclude that Plato equates appearance with art. Since, too, appearance resembles in some way the reality it "participates" in, one is forced to realize that for Plato art is always representational. It pictures something distinct from itself. If we ask what it pictures, the answer is obvious: reality. Thus reality stands in the same relation to art as it does to appearance, and this means that it must be described as the truly natural as well. As distinct from art, it can only be Nature. The troublesome contrast between art and nature is overcome with the help of the distinction between the human and the divine, but it surfaces again as identical to the distinction between the apparent and the real. The truly Natural for Plato, the realm of *physis*, is the Parmenidean reality of eternal rest; the merely artificial, the realm of *nomos*, is the Platonic appearance of temporal motion divided into the conventions of man and god. To keep the conventions of god clearly defined from reality, I will use *nature* when referring to the first and apply *Nature* to the second.

It is important to realize that Plato succeeds in undermining the two skeptical contrasts that bother him only because the equations hold between reality and Nature and appearance and art. Appearance succeeds in being appearance—that is, something more than sheer illusion—just for the reason that it is art. It somehow represents reality as an artist's picture represents a model. It thereby acquires to a certain degree the properties of reality and becomes, to the same degree, intelligible. If appearance were not representational art, it would not "participate" in the real and the intelligible; it would then lapse into being the sheer illusion Parmenides claimed the moving world to be, not appearance at all. Similarly, it is precisely because reality is a true Nature that the invidious contrast of Antiphon between the laws of convention and the laws of an apparent nature must fail. If only what is eternal and at rest is Nature, then the moving cosmos has to be redescribed as divine art. But in that case what Antiphon, Callicles, Diogenes, and other nihilists Plato opposed called the laws of nature are just as much matters of convention as the codes of civilized conduct they condemned for their unnaturalness. The two distinctions—one ontological, the other teleological—between the apparent and the real and the human and the divine therefore cooperate to relieve the skeptical issues that underlie Plato's work. Their cooperation ties together virtually the whole of his doctrines from the fields of metaphysics and epistemology to psychology, aesthetics, and political theory.

Before moving to identify the key elements of those doctrines, and to examine the strands of argument that unite them, it will be well to summarize the views I have expressed on Plato's ambitions as a philosopher. I have said that, in effect, he takes for granted crucial aspects of two disquieting, skeptical motifs. In saying that he accepts them I mean that he takes them seriously and on their own terms. He thinks that by using logic alone Zeno and Parmenides identified a genuine difficulty with the concept *motion*—a difficulty that is not to be solved by relying on an empiricist theory of meaning and knowledge, a difficulty, indeed, that is not to be solved in full at all, only mitigated. The moving cosmos, he agrees, is not fully intelligible. He thinks, too, that Antiphon and others presented a genuine moral and political issue when they identified ordinary morality as a matter of convention—an issue that is not to be resolved by upholding the merits of art over nature, an issue, indeed, that is not to be resolved completely, only tempered. The true home of the soul, he agrees, is a realm of Nature apart from the world. He thus starts his philosophical work from within the camp of those I have described as scientific and moral skeptics. Plato's description of reality as unmoving, intelligible Nature reflects his commitment to the key principles of that camp, wherein rest and right are associated with the real and the natural.

Yet Plato has commitments elsewhere, and so he seeks an escape from the nihilistic implications usually drawn from his principles. Essential to his planning is the replacement of the invidious contrasts of his fellow philosophers with distinctions of his own, which are still invidious, but no longer fully contrasting. For the contrast of Parmenides and Zeno between the illusory and the real, he substitutes his ontological distinction between the apparent and the real; for the contrast of Antiphon and Callicles between the artificial and the natural, he substitutes his distinction between the conventions of man and god. His two distinctions mesh through the equation of appearance with pictorial art. In these ways what was first in opposition becomes joined by bonds of similarity. The moving, apparent world of time resembles a fully real eternity by somehow picturing it; and what we call nature is like our culture in being a form of art. Thus one could say that Plato's ontological and teleological dualities serve both to link him to and to separate him from a skeptical position. We do live, they acknowledge, in a culture based on art, and in a world of sensory appearance that is not fully coherent. If we could, it would be better and more intelligible to live and to think apart from art and appearance altogether in a realm of Nature and reality. Just because the whole of appearance is pictorial art, however, we cannot in this life make an escape to nature. We can, then, defend the city-state as our proper, interim home. For the same reason we can, if only to a certain extent, understand our world as the likeness it is of the fully coherent. We cannot, then, denigrate empirical experience as illusory. Plato's description of appearance as moving, pictorial art reflects his commitment to the key objections that can be made to the scientific and moral nihilism of those who, like himself, equated the natural with the right and the real with the unmoving. His account of appearance thus amounts to the justification of the style of life of the urban intellectual that he was.

When Plato's descriptions of appearance as changeable art and of reality as unchanging Nature are seen as essential to an effort to reconcile a duality of commitments, everything I want to say about his ambitions as a philosopher should be clear. He wanted, first, to associate himself with the premises of those who held that only the indivisible and the motionless are real, but without accepting their scientific nihilism. He wanted, second, to associate himself with the premises of those who held that only the natural is just, but without accepting their moral nihilism. To return to my original description of his work, the difference between his account of reality and his account of appearance represents the distance between a solar core of skeptical, disquieting motifs and a planetary belt of orbiting doctrines designed to justify both empirical science and urban civilization.

For the most part Plato drew his account of reality from the work of Parmenides and other traditional sources. He was also indebted to others for certain aspects of his account of appearance; the philosophers Democritus and Gorgias had, for example, compared sensory qualities to the conventions of art before Plato wrote anything. Still, he was the designer of the essential notion that appearance—although often falling short of its potential—somehow "partakes" of reality and Nature. His escape from skepticism depends on an ability to apply that notion of participation to the cosmos. Before anything else, he had to make a case that the changeable world of sensory experience is analogous to a work of pictorial art that partially acquires the qualities of its subject. I now want to examine how he made that case.

1

Metaphysics–The Artifice of Time and Change

The Origin of the World: Two Cosmogonic Motifs

In the *Timaeus* Plato sets out to survey the sources of change and to plot the origin of what he calls particulars, or the fleeting objects of sensory awareness that are forever shifting about and varying themselves. He also ventures to explain how particulars are related to an unchanging world that always is and never, as he puts it, becomes. These are tasks he undertakes with qualms. He is convinced that the only knowable entities belong to the world of what is and does not become—entities he calls Forms and describes as unchanging, insensible objects of thought. He is also convinced that the only certain statements are those depicting relations between the Forms. Empirical accounts, dealing as they do with a subject matter on which nothing but opinions can be entertained, are necessarily imprecise, deficient, and, at best, mere likely stories (29 C). Likewise, any philosophical account of the relation between empirical particulars and the intelligible Forms must be less than fully coherent. If only the Forms can be spoken of in truth, then neither a changeable particular nor its relation to a Form can be described with total accuracy. A determined scientist who remained true to his calling would not concern himself with the world at all. Nonetheless, acknowledging the hardships he faces, Plato attempts to analyze physical change and to describe the relation between the moving cosmos and the permanent objects of thought that would, unlike the cosmos itself, form the subject matter of a true science.

As a first step toward finishing both tasks Plato argues that all change involves the making of something new out of a permanent, but indefinite, matter. To explain what he has in mind he points out that changeable shapes are imposed upon gold and wax in the modeling of figures made from those materials, and that changeable scents are received by the same inodorous base used in the making of diverse perfumes (50 A-C). Change is akin to manufacture in that whenever it occurs some new and unstable product is made from an already existing, neutral material. Thus, he concludes, analyses of change must be miniature cosmogonies—that is, they must explain the origin of newly created entities that collectively compose the world at any one moment. At this juncture Plato relies upon two very old and familiar cosmogonic motifs to complete his work. Both interpret change as the making of new sensory particulars by invisible, uncreated agents that always are and never become. Both, too, are derived from human productive acts. The key to an empirical understanding of change, in short, lies in understanding the philosophical relation of changeable particulars to the unchanging Forms. That relation, in turn, is elucidated by the ways in which human beings create.

In the passages cited Plato writes of a completely formless, neutral matter that is the recipient of all sensory qualities—of colors, tastes, and sounds as well as shapes and scents. He identifies this matter with space, saying that it is a vessel of becoming that holds the world. Perishable qualities appear and disappear on its surface, but it abides unaffected by any source of movement beyond it. Referring to the spatial vessel as "she," Plato goes on to explain that the particulars entering into her are wonderful and mysterious likenesses of eternal realities and that three natures are therefore to be distinguished: that which is made, that in which the making takes place, and that of which the things made are likenesses. Plato compares the receiving principle to a mother, the source to a father, and the intermediate nature they produce to a child (50 C-D).

Here Plato adapts to his theory of the Forms an archaic, pansexual cosmogony that takes the cosmos to be the offspring of two parents. According to that theory the entities that make up reality and that serve as the subject matter of true science have no spatial or temporal dimensions; they also lack all sensory qualities. They are, however, causally related to perceptible appearances in space and time. In these passages they have the status of male consorts to a single female receptacle. Their sexual prowess is said to be responsible for the fleeting qualities of appearance that gestate in the figurative womb of space. Thus the relation between the changing cosmos and its permanent cause is akin to that of mortal half siblings to an invisible, polyandrous mother and her equally invisible lovers. All change is a form of birth wherein only what is sired and is born, not what sires and bears, is visible.

That Plato is adapting, not uncritically adopting, a pansexual cosmogony is shown by a quick and serious lapse in his text from biological realism. There is, he writes, no union of the parents of becoming. The paternal Forms remain apart from the maternal receptacle of space, immune to change; only their mortal progeny touch the mother of becoming (51 E - 52 B). This biological oddity in

Plato's account is compounded by a further claim that appearances, as the children of reality, owe all their sensory features to the remote paternal Forms, receiving nothing but a position in space and time from their mother, who is, however close, without specific features of her own to impart to anything.

The reason for Plato's lapses from biological realism is that he includes the elements of a second cosmogonic motif in his account. He writes that the children of reality are likenesses of their male parents and so have their fathers' names, thereby making language applicable to both reality and appearance, Forms and particulars. His description suggests that they are to be construed as images of their fathers, and that they rest upon a featureless, mirrorlike surface that mysteriously reflects the qualities of unseen objects beyond it. This suggestion is strengthened by Plato's often choosing to illustrate, in other dialogues as well as the *Timaeus* itself, the relationship of appearances to reality as that of a set of ephemeral, moving images to a single, abiding model that both causes and identifies them. The comparison of a particular to an image is the figurative illustration that is the central object of debate in the *Parmenides* (132 D), for example, where the apparent membership of empirically similar things in a class is construed as a representational relation holding between the apparent members and a single Form they all resemble. Plato uses the same comparison in the *Cratylus* (439 A - B) where he indicates how Forms and the empirical sounds of speech are related. It appears in the *Phaedo* (76 D-E) and in the *Republic* (509 E - 510 A) as well. In the *Statesman* (285 E) Plato compares empirical objects to images or representational patterns; and he does the same in the *Timaeus* itself (37 D; 46 A; 50 C; 92 C), before, after, and in those passages where he calls particulars the offspring of reality. The pictorial relation between reality and appearance gives to the Forms their epistemological as well as their ontological priority over particulars; for what an image represents serves to identify it, as subject matter identifies a map or portrait. We cannot understand what anything empirical is, Plato holds, until we understand what intelligible pattern it portrays. The world of being identifies the world of becoming.

The persistent comparison of particulars to images is the key feature of the second cosmogonic motif used in the *Timaeus*. Early in the dialogue Plato compares the cosmos to a divine artifact. He writes that it is made up of numerous representations, or likenesses, of ungenerated Forms and arranged upon the chaotic receptacle of space by a cosmic artisan, a *demiourgos* (28 A-B). Here Plato compares the paternal Forms to an artist's uncreated models; the maternal womb of space acquires the status of an artist's canvas; and the half siblings of appearance become portraits, not offspring, of reality. The cosmic artist responsible for the clarity and arrangement of the portraits looks to his unchanging, intelligible models and fashions the best moving, representational work of art his medium of space will allow. All change is now a form, not of birth, but of portraiture, wherein only the portrayal, not the portrayed, is visible.

Plato appears to borrow both of his accounts of change from archaic cosmogonies that trace movement to the factors illustrated by either man's sexual or artistic powers. He uses both as merely metaphorical illustrations of how the relation between intelligible Forms and sensory particulars is to be grasped. He admits that they are not fully satisfactory illustrations, for the relation they are meant to clarify is, unlike that of parent to child or model to image, ineffable (*Timaeus* 51 B). There is nothing to indicate that in Plato's view space is alive or that all Forms are besouled, as literal parents of change would have to be. Nor is the comparison of the world to a representational artifact without severe limits of its own; the world's models are not sensory ones, as the models of normal portraits are; having no spatial dimensions they are not spatially apart from their pictures, either; and the space-canvas must be construed as a three-dimensional substratum of scents and sounds as well as of visual images.

Yet these two illustrations are the only ones Plato uses. They are clearly chosen by him for a purpose. Just as clearly they guide his thinking on the most important topics he discusses. Since, too, the difficulty Plato finds in stating exactly what the relation is between appearance and reality may arise from his use of them, they may not merely fall short of the task they are put to but create the problem. If, for example, all things in the world, including language, really were to picture only the Forms, then that would explain why the relation of a Form to something other than a Form could not be spoken of. The ineffable relation of appearance to reality would stem from the pictorial, but unpicturable, relation of word to object. For these reasons Plato's cosmogonic metaphors warrant scrutiny.

The Compatibility of Reproduction with Portraiture

A major point to notice about Plato's metaphors is that they result in an analogy between contrasting accounts of change. They use a different number of causes to explain the origin of sensible things, and they derive from opposed productive processes, one artificial the other natural. Their intermingling therefore raises issues of their compatibility and of their order of priority in the mind of Plato.

At a first hearing of the evidence the two metaphors are discordant, for to the three natures distinguished in the sexual analogy—the paternal Forms, a maternal receptacle, and their sensory progeny—the identification of the cosmos with divine art adds a fourth—a cosmic craftsman who is neither a parent nor a child of becoming. Plato, however, rids his speculations of any dissonance by, first, adding to his cosmology yet a fifth entity and, second, by giving to the receptacle of space a power that limits the productive role of the craftsman, allowing for his elimination as an independent source of particulars, although not of their design. In the end, the craftsman seems to stand for a figure who supervises a productive process without ever becoming a part of it.

Plato often compares the receptacle of space to a reflecting surface, such as that of a mirror (*Republic* 596 D), of a pool of water (*Republic* 510 A), or of a metallic edge (*Timaeus* 46 A). Thus it does not require the placing of pigments on it as an ordinary canvas does, and the Forms—posing as the models of the world—can cast images of themselves directly upon it without the help of an artist. They have this power only because a light source casts their profiles onto space. That source is the fifth entity Plato recognizes: the supreme, sunlike Form of the Good that illuminates the world of the Forms (*Republic* 508 E - 509 B). Because reality, with the help of the Good, creates its own portraits, there is no distinction between the *demiourgos's* pigments and the images he works with on the receptacle-canvas of space. To the extent that he fashions the cosmos, he works with a medium that is already a set of lighted pictures. Plato presents his task as that of sharpening some of their edges and making their disorderly motion more intelligent, so as to give better design and clearer purpose to at least the celestial regions of the world's preexistent imagery (*Timaeus* 30 A - B). His work may be compared to that of a projectionist in a motion picture theater, who makes neither the projected images, the film used, the light needed, nor the screen on which it is shown but merely focuses the lens and controls the movement of the patterns made by the equipment he operates.

Since the world is not a static set of pictures, and soul is the source of all movement for Plato (*Laws* 892 A; *Phaedrus* 245 E; *Phaedo* 99 B), some soul must start the movements the *demiourgos* directs. Since, too, movement is a form of change, and change has already been equated with creation, the *demiourgos*—who is himself a soul—must have some creative role as the governor of the world's celestial motion. It is, however, a minimally creative role. He can only manage the process of image production and thereby select, but not directly produce, the representations of reality that are to appear in the cosmos. The selective character of the cosmic artisan's power to create appears to be illustrated in the *Republic* (596 C-E), where an admittedly symbolic figure—there called a "marvelous sophist" as well as a *demiourgos*—is pictured as tilting what would seem to be the receptacle-mirror of space to catch reflections of different natures. Commentators on the *Republic* have usually associated Plato's "marvelous sophist" with an imitative, human painter who holds his mirror, as Hamlet did, up to nature.[1] But that interpretation is dubious. Plato calls his mirror-artist a *demiourgos*, or "by-culture-maker," and he is therefore distinct from any imitative artist using visible models, who is vehemently refused that title in the *Republic* (597 D), and who is called in the *Sophist* (235 B) an *eidolourgos*, or "by-image-maker." The "nature" the marvelous sophist holds his mirror up to would appear to be the true Platonic *physis*, the Forms, not the visible cosmos. In any event, the creation of imagery is here traced, not to an application of pigments to a canvas, but to a manipulation of a reflecting surface. That surface, therefore, has some creative power of its own, and so do the models it reflects. It

1. For example: James Adam, *The Republic of Plato*, 2 vols. (Cambridge: Cambridge University Press, 1902; rpt. 1965), 2: 389.

is by these means that changing images are produced; the artisan-soul who controls their production can be held responsible for their existence, yet he only controls the process that creates them and is not a part of it. If applied to procreation, the artisan-soul would become a breeder of stock—one who supervises the means of production without participating in it.

The limits to the causal power of the *demiourgos* do not imply that he does not really exist. Neither does anything else Plato says. In the *Timaeus* (33 C) there is a burlesque of the kind of anthropomorphic ideas of deity seemingly implied by a comparison of God to an artisan. The world fashioned by the *demiourgos* is there likened to a living organism and is later called a god (92 C). It is, however, a god without limbs or senses or digestive organs, there being no place for it to move to and nothing beyond it to see or eat. The element of burlesque in this account, plus the limits on the powers of the *demiourgos*, have sometimes been taken as showing that Plato was not really a theist and that there is, in the end, no artisan-god in his system.

The burlesque may well indicate, however, only Plato's express belief that soul is immaterial and distinct from the body. The agent-soul in a human body that can direct the muscles and fashion artifacts has no limbs of its own either, and no digestive organs, and no senses—privations that do not keep it from being an artisan. Indeed, if the *Epinomis* is a genuine work of Plato's, the soul is just that which can mold and make (981 B-C). As long as Plato's description of what a human soul is like is kept in mind, there is nothing in his burlesque to indicate that his anthropomorphism is not intended seriously or that the *demiourgos* is superfluous. Since the soul for Plato is what is uniquely human about us, his anthropomorphism is of a very special, highly doctrinal kind. What we and the *demiourgos* truly are is like the limbless, eyeless god the world is.

At the same time one must note that Plato is seriously interested in limiting the creative role of his *demiourgos*. In an effort to give a genuine, if mythical, significance to Plato's theism Cornford has held that there are no limitations on the creativity of the *demiourgos*. He has objected that the symbolism of the Forms' acting directly on the receptacle of space cannot be taken literally. In his view, the Forms can have no causal powers, for a static model and an unmoving reflecting surface can produce only a stable image. Since the cosmos is the world of becoming, there must be a principle of soul to set it in motion. Thus, Cornford concludes, the soul-*demiourgos* of the *Timaeus* symbolizes a causal principle that is central to Plato's position and that is responsible for the creation of all particulars.[2] The need to trace movement to the soul is clear, but that feature of Plato's cosmology is compatible with the symbolism granting the Forms power to act directly upon the receptacle. All that is necessary is that soul be given control over a mechanism that by itself casts static images; through its operation motion would be introduced to the world. In the allegory of the cave in the *Republic* attendants move manufactured articles back and forth in front of a fire, thereby creating moving images on the cave's wall. But the power to act upon the wall belongs to the fire, not to the cave attendants. Plato never suggests that the *demiourgos* creates the matter out of which he fashions the world; since the receptacle is just space, the matter he works with must be something else, for out of empty space nothing can be made. The *demiourgos* therefore needs pigments, but these are, for Plato, already images whose preexistent status in respect to the work of the *demiourgos* is stressed consistently (*Timaeus* 29 A; 52 D). Plato is wedded to the point that soul does not

2. Francis Cornford, *Plato's Cosmology* (New York: The Liberal Arts Press, 1957), pp. 28, 196-97.

directly create the world's imagery, for it is that point which allows his two cosmogonic metaphors to come together harmoniously. He has to limit in some way the creative power of his fourth cause: the soul-*demiourgos*. The Forms do act directly on the receptacle. Their causal powers, however, do not imply the superfluousness of soul. There is, in short, no good reason to think Plato does not mean everything he says about the powers of both the Forms and the soul-*demiourgos*. His doctrines are fully compatible. There is no need to choose between a Form-created world and a soul-created world. The artisan-soul who fashions the time-measuring firmament does so by bringing clarity to a preexistent set of images that the Forms themselves have made.

Given the point that both the *demiourgos* and the Forms have causal powers, the relations between the metaphysical and empirical entities that Plato recognizes in his two cosmogonic motifs could be diagramed as follows:

Reality:	Forms	Models	Fathers
Appearance:	Particulars	Images	Children
Space:	Receptacle	Canvas-Mirror	Mother
Agency:	Soul	Artist	Animal Breeder

In addition to these four kinds of things, a fifth must be understood as acting as a light source on the canvas-mirror of space. That fifth entity is the object of supreme metaphysical importance: the Form of the Good, best symbolized by the sun.

The Priority of Portraiture over Reproduction

The divorce of the soul from the mechanism of creation clearly results in a linkage of the two cosmogonic metaphors of the *Timaeus*. The relation of child to mother and father is similar to that of picture to mirror and model. Taken together, they point to an equation of sexual with pictorial processes. Indeed, Plato's claim is the larger thesis that any distinction between natural and artificial modes of production is unjustified. How his thesis is to be understood depends upon the order of priority of the productive modes it equates. Pictorial, and therefore presumably artificial, processes might be equated with natural ones. On the other hand, sexual, and therefore presumably natural, processes might be equated with those of art. In primitive pansexual cosmogonies that ascribe to the world an origin in birth, the first equation often appears. The consummated marriage of earth and sky, Hesiod tells us, brought forth the cosmos. Appealing to the fertile union of Yin and Yang, Chuan Tzu credits to different, although similar, parents the same child. Other, less famous, and often anonymous authors of ancient texts describe coupling gods and goddesses, cosmic eggs that hatch, laboring wind-impregnated seas, stormlit sheets of sperm that fall as rain, and still other living agents of generation in their stories of how the world began. If procreation is the prototype of all becoming, then art, too, must be a form of sexuality. Thus it is a familiar practice for classical poets to invoke the muse of love before beginning their work which, like everything else, must arise from the creative force of eros. In contrast, the view of the world as a divine artifact would seem to rival in age and scope the pansexual cosmogonies of antiquity. Mircea Eliade is so impressed by the evidence that primitive societies throughout the world viewed all aspects of the cosmos as pictures having extra-worldly models that he writes of Plato as the philosopher of primitive religious mentality.[3] Ananda K. Coomaraswamy also stresses the affinity between Plato's

3. Mircea Eliade, *Cosmos and History: The Myth of the Eternal Return* (New York: Pantheon Books, 1954), p. 34.

exemplarism and ancient Indian cosmologies.[4] Any system that takes pictorial art as the prototype of all becoming must equate, in a manner opposite to that of the classical poet, sexuality with art.

Plato's intent in the way his own equation is to be understood must be gleaned primarily from dialogues other than the *Timaeus*, but he does make himself clear. In the *Sophist* (242 C-D) his spokesman ridicules pansexual cosmologies, and Plato himself makes no use of sexual analogies beyond what appears in the *Timaeus*, where he is trying to show the similarity of birth to portraiture. He stresses repeatedly, on the other hand, the thesis that nature is divine art. It is the prime thesis he uses to distinguish his position from materialistic schools of thought, which fail to recognize the primal status of foresight, design, and choice in the world. Accordingly, it expresses a point of view that he displays in his handling of virtually all the philosophical problems he felt he had to deal with. In the *Phaedo*, for instance, the famous discussion on the character and origin of knowledge is dominated by the implicit point that all the parts of nature are representational artifacts. Socrates there declares all knowledge to be a form of recollection; in response to a request for clarification of what he means, he says that when one recognizes and is able to identify an object, a mental picture of something previously seen is conjured up, and that is recollection. When one sees a portrait of Simmias, for instance, one may be reminded through a memory image of Simmias himself; if so, one will be able to identify the portrait as a portrait of Simmias, and so will "know" in a loose, empirical sense what it is. Empirical recollection of this sort is parallel to the way in which one acquires true knowledge of the world's models and a Form,

4. Ananda K. Coomaraswamy, "Vedic Exemplarism," *Harvard Journal of Asiatic Studies* 1 (1936): 44-64, 281.

not a sensory particular, is remembered; for in coming to know who the visible sitter for a portrait is, one will have to recollect his transcendent, invisible prototype.

Central to Socrates' argument is the claim that all aspects of the cosmos fall short of exemplifying exactly any concept. There are, he insists by way of example, no two empirical things of exactly equal length. The ability to recognize any sensory object as falling under a given concept thus requires an awareness of the actual, extrasensory subject matter of one's thoughts. Without such a transcendent awareness one would not be able to apply language to any aspect of appearance, for no empirical object can identify any other (*Phaedo* 76 C). Since there is no grasping of the transcendent Forms in this life, the soul's immortality and previous acquaintance with reality is presupposed by the ability to talk.

Socrates' account of knowledge, together with the argument for the preexistence of the soul that it supports, rests upon a comparison of sensory objects to portraits. The analogy he uses is one of seeing a more or less sketchy portrait and being reminded of its subject, previous acquaintance with whom is essential if one is to be able to recognize and name who it is that the portrait represents. Thus the relationship of appearance to reality, of the objects of vague sensation to those of exact thought, is that of portraiture to prototype. It is for this reason that Plato calls his cosmological account of the world in the *Timaeus* (29 B-D) a "likely story" (*eikos mythos*); it is about a mere likeness that has but a rough similarity to its transcendent subject matter. The soul of any true lover of knowledge, he remarks elsewhere, would be tempted to ignore the world's visible pictures altogether and not engage in empirical speculations; if, however, that temptation is resisted for fear of one's being deemed a madman, the soul's earthly loves will still be honored as but holy images of a divine realm (*Phaedrus* 251 A; *Statesman* 285 E).

In the *Republic* the two famous allegories of the cave and the divided line use different aspects of the thesis that nature is divine, representational art. Both serve as particularly vivid examples of how seriously Plato was committed to it. The allegory of the cave draws its dramatic force from a contrast between a *natural* world outside an occupied cavern and an *artificial*, humanly built world within. Beyond the cave's entrance there are shadows and reflections, the parts of nature that cast them, and the sun that supplies the light. Within, this same schema is repeated except that everything visible is artificially made. There are a kindled fire supplying artificial light, artifacts—including representational images of plants and animals as well as implements of all kinds—and their shadows cast upon a wall. Prisoners chained before these shadows are in an "unnatural" state of bondage. If freed from their chains by an educator and shown the artifacts above them, they would undoubtedly first find them strangely unreal. But if guided further up and out of the cave to their true, natural home—a journey symbolizing the passage of the soul from life to death—they would be forced to realize that their former estate was one of ignorance, and that they had been living in an unnatural world of illusory artifice. Since most of the visible objects above the ground have parallels beneath it, the point of the allegory is that what is normally thought of as natural—the sun, plants, animals, and shadows—is actually a world of artifacts, and that what is truly natural—the Forms—lies beyond the cosmos.

The allegory of the divided line uses a different contrast. In it the degrees of reality are symbolized by dividing a single line into four graded sections. The least real things, represented by the shortest length, are images (*eikones*), such as shadows (*skias*) and reflections (*phantasmos*). A longer length of line is granted to the objects that cast the images, and these are the supposedly nonrepresentational bodies of nature (*phyteuton*) and the manufactured products of art (*skeuaston*). In the third section of the line the originals of the second section appear again, but they are placed there by virtue of being treated as images of intelligible prototypes and are not considered as models themselves. The fourth and longest section of the line symbolizes the Forms that are the intelligible models of the images in the third section.

The contrast drawn is not between art and nature, but between *models* and *images*. The same contrast guides Plato's discussion of epistemology, which appears as part of the allegory. There is, he asserts, a possible study of images, of their empirical models, of those models treated as images of transcendent Forms, and of the Forms themselves. In the whole of his discussion only one contrast is drawn and only two kinds of entities set apart: models and images. The fourfold classification in ontology and epistemology arises only because the ordinary, empirical distinction between model and image is kept while it is at the same time given a symbolic significance as illustrating the relation of reality to appearance. Classed in terms of what kind of entities the allegory recognizes, everything must be either a Form or a particular, a transcendent prototype or a sensory image, whether treated as such or not. All studies, too, must lead to knowledge or to opinion, each with its own distinctive object (*Republic* 533 E).

Numerous writers, starting with Aristotle[5] and continuing to Copleston,[6] have held a different view of the allegory of the divided line. For them it is an allegory that illustrates

5. Aristotle, *Metaphysics* 987b 14 ff.
6. Frederick Copleston, *A History of Philosophy* (Garden City, N.Y.: Doubleday and Company, 1962), 1, Pt. 1: 179.

a fourfold division of objects into images, empirical models, numbers plus other mathematical and geometric entities, then the Forms. Their interpretation of Plato's intent blurs the distinction between appearance and reality by dividing the objects of sensation and thought into four, not two, categories. Plato's thinking, however, is dualistic, not quadrifid, and there is nothing in his discussion of the divided line to warrant a different conclusion. Although the line has four sections, its only contrast is between models and images—a contrast that involves but two terms and that illustrates no relation but that of reality to appearance. One must bear in mind that in Plato's allegory a metaphysical relation is illustrated with the help of an empirical contrast that is, of itself, obvious but without metaphysical significance. Thus to the uninitiate there seems to be an important difference between shadows and the objects that cast them. To the initiate, however, all sensible objects are basically alike—even though distinguishable—and the only important contrast is between intelligible Forms and empirical particulars. Plato does not contrast, he compares empirical models to their shadows. Likewise, he does not contrast, he compares the true objects of geometrical and mathematical study to the Forms. He is, clearly, a dualist.

Taken together, the two allegories of the divided line and the cave present the cosmos as representational art. The divided line interprets all sensory particulars as representations either of other particulars or of the Forms, and the cave makes it clear that it is an artificial, not a natural, mode of representation that is meant. In the *Sophist* (265 E - 266A) Plato offers what amounts to a formal definition of nature as divine art, which must be taken in both senses. There his spokesman lays down the principle that the products of nature, as they are called, are works of divine art and that things made by men are works of human art. These two kinds of art are then further divided into the making of originals and the making of imitations, so that everything empirical is grouped into four kinds of art.

The teleological contrast Plato draws between human and divine production is a principle of classification that follows the ontological contrast in the allegory of the cave between an artificial, humanly constructed interior world and an exterior realm of nature. It does not correspond to that allegory completely, of course, for divine art is there nonexistent. The only artifacts mentioned are man-made; the artificial character of the cavern world would otherwise be blurred. The definition of nature as divine art, however, formalizes the symbolic message of the allegory: the cosmos, symbolized by the cave, is an artifact. Since the representational artifacts of plants and animals in the cave, although man-made, both stand for nature symbolically as they represent it literally, the definition of the *Sophist* must be taken to mean that what we call nature is divine, representational art—a definition in full harmony with all aspects of Plato's metaphysics. Indeed, his metaphysical, invisible entities—souls, Forms, space, and the Good as a light source—are precisely those presupposed by the existence of a representational work of art.

Clearly, the linkage of sexual with artistic creativity in the *Timaeus* is to be understood as an equation of natural with artificial creation, not the reverse. Plato's thesis is that biological reproduction and growth are artistic processes. Elements of an archaic, pansexual cosmology appear in his account only to the extent necessary for him to illustrate his point. It is incumbent upon anyone who would claim that art is the basis of all becoming to show how procreation—being the most likely choice of a counterexample and the prototype of what natural generation is normally taken to be—may be seen as a kind of artistry. That is the point of the duality of cosmogonic metaphors in the *Timaeus* where, with impressive ingenuity, Plato shows how a father of becoming can be its model, and how the womb of generation can be its canvas-mirror, and how, therefore, the cycle of animate procreation that is but a part of cosmic change can be living portraiture. Time itself, Plato claims, is but a moving, multiple image of eternity. Part of the means used to portray eternity is procreation, for that is the way all men come to partake of immortality (*Laws* 721 B-C). By succession of generations the race abides as time's equal twin and companion, and so shares in the stability of eternity. Sexuality is a form of artistry.

Indeed, the means by which all appearance is generated and sustained are those of art. It is man's artistic powers that illustrate the whole of becoming, that explain change best, and that provide the greatest insight into how appearance is related to reality. All the grand, fair, and primary things of the world are not, as the materialists believe, products of nature and chance, of the hard and the soft and the light and the heavy mindlessly pushing and pulling each other; they are, Plato insists, works of art and design, of soul and choice (*Laws* 889 A - 892 A; *Phaedo* 99 B). The entire realm of appearance is purposeful, living art. Aimless principles of mechanical causation do work within it, but they can only transmit, not start, motion of their own (*Timaeus* 46 D-E). Consequently, they remain the obliging ministers of design (*Timaeus* 46 C-D); and the point stands that all that is primal and basic to the moving cosmos arises from the foresight, wisdom, and artistry of soul.

It should now be clear why Plato wanted to identify the world with appearance and appearance with art. It should also be clear how, through an equation of sexuality with portraiture, he went about making those identifications. His metaphysics in both its ontological and teleological dimensions is to be understood as the result of his efforts in this basic matter. I next want to begin the task of showing in some detail how Plato uses his cosmology to divorce himself from skeptical conclusions on the intelligibility of empirical science and the justice of conventional morality and urban life.

2

Epistemology—The Identification of the Artificial by the Natural

A Parallel between Theories of Thought and Culture

When giving to his Forms a power to act directly on the receptacle of space to create particulars, Plato is careful to limit their work as to be able to say that the world of appearance is an incomplete and imperfect version of reality. Not all Forms are reflected in the world (*Statesman* 286 A); the principle of soul selects only some for portrayal. Those Forms which are allowed to reflect themselves do not succeed in re-creating in full the features they have; the created nature of appearance prevents Forms, even with the help of the *demiourgos*, from creating particulars that are exactly like themselves (*Timaeus* 37 D).

These two limits on the causal powers of the Forms are basic to almost everything Plato has to say about both science and civilization. If the divine art work of the world is incomplete and imperfect, then the civilizing arts of man can be justified in terms of the possibility open to them of adding to and aiding what already has been created.

Likewise, it is possible to justify the priority of thought over sensation without condemning empirical judgments as utterly false. Thought, taking the full complement of the Forms as its subject, can be viewed as a complete and exact vehicle of knowledge—a vehicle that does not clash with sensation, but supplements and clarifies its limited, distorted testimony. The incomplete and imperfect status of the world's art allows, in short, for analogous doctrines on how nature, so called, is related to culture and how sensation is related to thought. In each case these analogous doctrines serve to keep intact the priority of thought and nature over sensation and convention, while still justifying empirical science and a certain kind of culture Plato associates with the city-state. In this chapter I will examine, by way of Plato's theory of language, his views on the relation of sensation to thought.

The Incomplete and Imperfect Standing of Empirical Science

Limited as they are in their work, the Forms for Plato still have a causal priority over the particulars they create. Their causal priority is also an epistemological priority. They are the objects of knowledge; their participant particulars are the objects of opinion (*Phaedrus* 247 C). In explaining his doctrine Plato notes that whereas knowledge is related to ignorance as the real is related to the nonexistent, it is related to opinion as the real is related to the apparent (*Republic* 477 A-B). Thus there are three ontological and three epistemological states Plato recognizes. Knowledge pertains to what is real: the Forms; ignorance pertains to what is not: nothing at all; opinion pertains to what lies between the real and the nonexistent: appearance. Since appearance is an incomplete and imperfect version of reality, Plato's set of parallels between his ontology and his epistemology invites the obvious inference that opinion is an incomplete and imperfect version of knowledge. Because opinion has as its province the world of sensory experience, what we call empirical science is for Plato a partial, defective version of a true science of thought, which takes the Forms for its subject.

Why empirical science is incomplete is clear. There are many subjects we can have knowledge of, Plato points out, that may have no empirical dimension. The industrial inventor, for example, could have knowledge of tools—such as a spindle—even if none should exist empirically (*Cratylus* 389 B). Likewise, we can know what a just state would be like even though history provides us with no full examples (*Republic* 592 B). The ability of a knowing person to invent or to discuss whatever is not yet empirically extant shows that a purely empirical science must be less than universal in scope. The objects of sense are bound to be fewer in number than the objects of thought.

Nothing Plato says contradicts his view that appearance and opinion are incomplete versions of reality and knowledge. Still, his doctrine has sometimes been ignored. The major reason it has been is that according to the *Timaeus* (30C) the cosmos pictures all Forms of living creatures. There is, then, no possibility of new species of plant and animal life's appearing in the future. Nature is complete. The claim that all biological Forms are represented in the world amounts to a rejection by Plato of evolutionary theories current in his time—theories otherwise compatible with his metaphysics. When coupled with the doctrine that the Forms act directly upon the receptacle of space to produce sensory images, Plato's rejection of evolution can seem to imply that all the Forms necessarily manifest themselves in appearance. Such, at any rate, is the conclusion Lovejoy arrives at in his *The Great Chain of Being*.

Lovejoy begins his book by claiming that the fundamental and antithetical distinction in all well-formed classifications of religion is between "this worldly and other worldly" forms. When he tries to classify Plato's doctrines in terms of this distinction, he finds he cannot do so. Rather than take the difficulty he finds as posing a possible challenge to his views, he decides that Plato displays a duality of incompatible religious tendencies; and he does not hesitate to read into the dialogues contradictory tenets. He argues that one of Plato's deities, the Form of the Good, is transcendent and otherworldly while a second, the *demiourgos* of the *Timaeus*, is immanent and this-worldly. To bridge the gap between them Plato formulates a doctrine that becomes, Lovejoy holds, that of the great chain of being—a chain linking reality to appearance in Neoplatonic philosophy. A transcendent Form, Lovejoy argues, has the essential attribute of exemplifying itself in appearance.[1] If all Forms do have this attribute, then appearance is not an incomplete version of reality, and opinion is not an incomplete version of knowledge.

Although understandable, Lovejoy's views are obviously inadmissible. Not all Forms are reflected in appearance (*Statesman* 286 A; *Cratylus* 389 B; *Republic* 592 B). Even though the Forms act directly upon space, it is through the selective art of a designer—akin to that of a man tilting a mirror or moving shapes before a firelit wall—that the world arises. The Forms cannot reflect themselves without the help of soul; and if all biological Forms are, as a matter of fact, permanently pictured, that only indicates that Plato

1. A. O. Lovejoy, *The Great Chain of Being* (Cambridge, Mass.: Harvard University Press, 1936), pp. 51-52.

views culture as a second order of creation that introduces novelty to the world. "Nature" may be complete, but that fact does not imply that the whole of appearance is a complete representation of reality. The "great chain of being" applied to Plato is as faulty as the supposed antithesis it is invented to link. If this world is representational art, then of course there is another world that it pictures—that, however, is a matter of simple inference, not of religious and metaphysical indecision. Plato's theistic doctrines are not contradictory; there is no gap in his views he is obliged to bridge; and he does not hold that a Form necessarily manifests itself in appearance. For him the world is an incomplete representation of the Forms, to which man may add. An empirical science is for that reason also incomplete.

But if it is clear why sensation cannot be as broad as thought, it is not immediately clear why it cannot be as certain. Not all science is empirical, but that point does not support Plato's claim that nothing empirical can be known. There are many empirical propositions, so we all believe, that we know to be true or false. Why, then, does Plato argue in the manner he does? In trying to answer this question one might be tempted to suppose that Plato has a queer, exalted view of knowledge that is foreign to, or more strict than, ordinary views on what it is to know something, and that he therefore doesn't do anything so preposterous as to deny the possibility of what we would call empirical knowledge. After all, he does admit that men have more than mere belief about such things as the roads they have taken (*Meno* 97 A) and the events they have witnessed (*Theaetetus* 201 B). In an effort to reduce the air of paradox about Plato's texts, Crombie has argued that for Plato the word *knowledge (episteme)* is reserved for a kind of understanding that exceeds in depth and clarity the understanding we ordinarily have and call knowledge. Thus there is only a semantic, not doctrinal, division between Plato's views and ordinary convictions. He does not have, Crombie insists, any special desire to tell us that—in ordinary English—we cannot have knowledge of empirical fact.[2]

An interpretation of Plato along these lines may be reassuring to those who like to think of him as a man with whom they might possibly agree, but it will not do as a description of his position. Men do properly distinguish between judgments based on their own experience and judgments based on the unreliable testimony of others; still, although they may think otherwise, that is a distinction internal to the province of opinion, not of knowledge. Any enlightened person would recognize that there is as great a gap between true knowledge and opinion as there is between firsthand experience and secondhand testimony. Nothing empirical can be known. Plato does deny—in our own, ordinary terms—that we can know anything empirical. He accepts the view of Socrates, who was executed because, among other things, he went about Athens denying that such famous and accomplished men as Homer, Solon, and Pericles ever knew anything about poetry or law. It emasculates Plato's theory of knowledge not to see it as a genuine affront to ordinary conviction. In his view empirical beliefs really are as defective as they are incomplete. Yet he has no exalted views of knowledge. The reason empirical judgments are defective is that they are never true. We cannot know what isn't true, for a proof of the falsity of an opponent's assertion is always a refutation of his claim to know. Yet for Plato all empirical claims are untrue. Indeed, they not only are but must be untrue. Thus empirical science can never be a vehicle of knowledge.

To understand Plato's views on the difference between opinion and knowledge it is necessary to examine his theory

2. I. M. Crombie, *An Examination of Plato's Doctrines*, 2 vols. (London: Routledge and Kegan Paul, 1963), 2: 135.

of language. It is a theory that parallels his ontology and that dictates the conclusion that empirical claims can aspire to the status of opinion but nothing more. Plato conceives of language as composed of names. Adjectives and verbs are like proper nouns in that they all, he thinks, name something. Most men assume that these names have as their bearers sensible objects. That is a mistake, however, which stems from the worldly use we put language to—a mistake reflecting cavernous ignorance and giddy confusion (*Republic* 515 B; *Cratylus* 439 C). The actual bearer of a word-name is an indestructible, intelligible Form. The ability of a word to retain a meaning when it has no empirical bearer shows that this must be so. The word *spindle*, for example, would still have meaning if all empirical spindles were destroyed. Thus *spindle*, *large*, and *just* name for Plato The Spindle, The Large, and The Just. Other words name other Forms.

In the *Cratylus* Plato discusses the relationship of words to their bearers. His chief concern is to refute the notion that convention or stipulation alone creates the link between name and named. There is nothing either right or wrong, true or false, about a stipulation. Thus there would be nothing to choose between calling a man a man or calling him a horse if stipulation sufficed to link words with their objects (*Cratylus* 385 A-B). It is true, however, that a man is a man and false that he is a horse. A conventional theory of language therefore does not account for our obvious ability to say something true as well as something false (*Cratylus* 385 B-C). Names must be more than applied to their objects; they must also apply.

One might object to Plato's argument on the ground that he does not distinguish sufficiently naming from asserting, and that whereas assertions are true or false, namings are not. Plato would appear, however, to have a rather sophisticated view of language that is designed to equate naming with asserting. Whenever we refer to something, his point seems to be, we make use of its name; but in order for a name to refer, it must describe. It cannot pick out or identify its referent unless it, in effect, gives a true account of what its referent is like. If it did not give a true account, it would be a mere noise, not a significant part of speech. Truth is a prerequisite for reference; reference is not, as conventionists assume, the prerequisite for truth. Meaning and truth, one might say, are prior to denotation or reference. It is with a failure to recognize these facts that Plato taxes a conventional theory of language. Thus naming is a form of referring, and referring is a form of describing; but to describe is also to assert that a thing is of a certain kind; consequently, there is no cardinal difference between naming and asserting.

The principle Plato draws from his conclusion is that words describe accurately the Forms they refer to. The Large is large and The Just is just. If these Forms did not have the features they are the Forms for, then the words *large* and *just* would not refer to them, and so not be their names. If, too, these same Forms only sometimes had the features they are the Forms for, then only sometimes would their names succeed in functioning as names. Thus Plato postulates an eternal set of Forms that forever warrant the descriptive names they bear. The Beautiful is always beautiful; The Good is always good; and every other eternal Nature is always what it needs to be to deserve its name (*Cratylus* 439 D-440 B). As a postulate, this doctrine may have its problems and fail to convince everyone, Plato admits (*Cratylus* 440 B-C; *Phaedo* 100 A-B). He thinks it is the best available theory, however, and one worth as sturdy a defense as he can muster.

It is because the Forms, by hypothesis, have all the features that make possible successful reference that they are for Plato the objects of knowledge. Successful reference is a form of true description, and truth is the essential feature of knowledge. The way Plato develops his point is to say that our concepts, which coincide with the sense of our words, apply in full to the Forms. Reality, indeed, is to be defined in linguistic terms as precisely that to which our concepts truly apply. The Form Triangle, for example, is something real just because it fits the concept we have of a triangle; it is truly triangular. The Forms Beautiful and Good are also realities for the reason that they are genuinely beautiful and good. Thus reality for Plato is the subject of a true proposition, or *logos*. "The Triangle is triangular" is true, and the reason it is true is that it predicates triangularity of a true, that is a real, triangle. The truth of a proposition of this kind makes knowledge possible, for knowledge in Plato's view is knowledge that a given proposition is true.

It is because particulars do not have all the features that make possible successful reference that they are for Plato the objects of opinion. They are distorted versions of the Forms, and so our concepts do not truly apply to them. When out of a desire or need to talk of the world we apply a concept to a particular, the result is an untrue *mythos* in which a partial failure of reference occurs. Like speakers in a dimly lit cave filled with shadows, we may think we refer successfully to the unstable representations of life about us, but the actual referent of everything we say lies beyond our sight and hearing (*Republic* 515 B-C). What we call a plant is only the shadow of a plant; thus the word *plant* really refers to something unseen. The same is true of all other words. The visible, three-sided figure we are likely to call a triangle, for example, never will fit, no matter how precisely drawn, Euclid's definition of a triangle. Likewise, no line drawn tangentially to a circle will touch but one point on the circle's circumference and so succeed in being a true tangent. These drawings are but approximations to the extra-worldly triangle and tangent to which our words actually refer (*Republic* 510 B). Thus a failure of reference is also a failure of truth. Since our words do not refer to particulars, particulars cannot be adequately described. They are appearances, not realities. Appearance, indeed, is to be defined linguistically as that to which our concepts do not fully apply. For this reason it is unknowable. Strictly speaking, everything we try to say about the world is untrue. Consequently, an empirical judgment, or *mythos*, never expresses knowledge. That is why Plato is reluctant to offer a cosmology in the *Timaeus*. It is probably his reason, too, for describing the relation between appearance and reality as ineffable. Our language does not permit us to say precisely how Forms are related to similar, but defective particulars, for we can neither genuinely refer to nor truly describe anything that isn't a Form.

In failing to be true, an empirical judgment is not so defective as to warrant being labeled false. Calling two more or less equal sticks equal may not display knowledge, but it doesn't display total ignorance either (*Meno* 97 B; *Symposium* 202 A). The two sticks are, in appearance, equal. Thus Plato justifies calling them equal as the expression of a "true opinion" or "true belief." Likewise, the error involved in calling an empirical triangle a triangle is unlike the grosser error of calling it a circle or square. The empirical triangle comes close to fitting the concept of triangularity in a way empirical circles and squares do not. We are, then, justified in calling it a triangle, even though it isn't really what we say it is. *Triangle* neither applies nor fails to apply to visible, three-sided plane figures. We use that word, Plato's point is, only "mythologically" when discussing chalk lines on slates. We are discussing a figure that neither is nor isn't a triangle—a figure, in short, that is an apparent triangle. Thus the law of noncontradiction does not apply to appearance. That is why it is appearance and why it is unknowable.

As being is to becoming, so truth is to opinion (*Timaeus* 29 C). As becoming, or appearance, lies between what is real and what does not exist at all, so opinion lies between the true and the false.

The set of parallels between Plato's ontology, epistemology, and linguistic theory can be summed up as follows: reality is the object of thought and knowledge and can be described in a true proposition, or *logos*, that corresponds to what is; nothing at all is the province of ignorance and can be described only in a false proposition that must, obviously, fail to correspond to anything; appearance, lying between the the real and the unreal, is the object of opinion and sensation and can be described only in a defective proposition, or *mythos*, that corresponds only in part to its subject, thereby being neither true nor false. This summation should make clear why, for Plato, empirical science is an imperfect, not merely an incomplete, discipline. The language we must use to report the results of inquiry does not allow us to refer to or describe in full accuracy the world of sensory appearance. No matter what we say, we must in Plato's view be a little wrong.

Recollection and the Judgments of Sense and Thought

When he taxes empirical science, or true opinion, with being as incomplete in scope and as imperfect in status as the realm of appearance it takes as its province, Plato is careful not to indict it entirely. It does not stand in contradiction to a true, complete science with Forms as subjects. There is much it can investigate, and its reports cannot be dismissed as false. It is merely an incomplete and imperfect version of knowledge. Thus empirical judgments do not conflict with intelligible judgments, and there is no serious clash between what the eye attests to and what the mind says must be so. The relation of sense to thought is not the relation of the illusory to the real, but of the apparent to the real.

As a way of showing how empirical judgments, although strictly untrue, harmonize with intelligible judgments, Plato develops his famous doctrine of anamnesis, or recollection. When we see two more or less equal sticks we are reminded, he argues, of the Form Equality, which we must have beheld in a former life. With the help of that reminiscence we apply to its participants a concept that truly applies only to a Form, saying of the two sticks that they are equal. Since we have but one language to talk of both reality and appearance, the meaning of our empirical judgment is the same as the meaning of the intelligible judgment "Equality Itself is equal." The only difference is that one judgment is true; the other is less than strictly true without being strictly false. One of the basic points about Plato's doctrine is that all empirical references are made with the help of intelligible concepts. We cannot describe the world except in terms that apply to the Forms. Our language thus weds us to descriptions of the objects of sense that do not differ in meaning from, and do not contradict, our descriptions of the objects of thought. If, without thinking at all, we could formulate a judgment on the basis of sense experience alone, we might find a cardinal discrepancy in meaning and truth value between what we judge to be so when we think and what we judge to be so when we observe. To talk of the world at all, however, we have to rely on concepts gained from a previous life and derived from some kind of intellectual, not empirical, experience. We cannot, therefore, generate a serious conflict between the testimonies of sense and thought. The testimony of sense just is, by way of recollection and a common language, the testimony of thought used in a realm where it ceases to be fully true but without becoming fully false. Thus Plato divorces himself from the position of Parmenides and Zeno, wherein thought and sense are taken to be at odds in their verdicts. The judgments of sense are dependent on the judgments of thought—just as sensory particulars themselves are dependent upon the intelligible Forms. What we think of the Forms, Nature, always identifies what we experience as the particulars of art. The priority of thought over sensation thus results, not in a dismissal of the empirical, but in its partial assimilation to the intelligible. This point is basic to Plato's position. In his own way he is an extreme Parmenidean who uses the priority of thought over sensation to overcome the supposed full duality between them. The Parmenidean antithesis between sensation and thought is, so Plato's position amounts to, an antithesis that cannot be stated or even conceived. Because what we sense is identified by what we think, there can be no contradiction between the testimony of eye and mind. The eye borrows its language, so to speak, from the mind; and with what is borrowed nothing can be said that is not sanctioned by the lender.

The "Third Man" and a Problem in Plato's Theory of Language

The role of Plato's Forms in both causing and identifying the particulars that participate in them indicates in the strongest possible way that they have the properties they are the Forms for. The Equal Itself could not cause its participants to be more or less equal unless it were itself equal. Neither could it lend its name to its participants unless it deserved what it lends. Thus each Form has the property it is the Form for. Each is, so to speak, self predicating. That principle is a crucial feature of Plato's philosophy. He clearly accepts it in a fully conscious manner. In the *Phaedo* (74 B), for example, he claims that we can acquire our concepts only from what they truly apply to: the Forms. We cannot have gained the concept *equality* from observing merely more or less equal sticks; since we don't behold anything in this life that fits our concepts exactly, our use of a language implies the prior existence of our souls in a realm where we could learn the meaning of what we say. Plato's account of concept formation and his argument for the immortality of the soul rest on the explicit tenet that the Forms have the properties they are the Forms for.

In spite of the abundant clarity on the general principle that a Form has the property it is the Form for, a significant number of Plato's commentators have argued otherwise. It is easy to see why. Plato's position here is like that he holds on the impossibility of empirical knowledge; it seems too obviously absurd to be the position of an intelligent man. Surely, one would like to say, some concepts and words do apply to empirical things. Maybe geometrical concepts never fit perfectly the somewhat irregular shapes we apply them to, but mathematical and temporal concepts would seem to be different. A single moving particular is truly described as one moving particular—or so it would seem. Even more to the point, surely some words and concepts cannot apply to timeless and spaceless things like the Forms. The Large, The Red, Equality Itself, and Motion Itself cannot, it seems obvious, be large, red, equal, and moving. Only things with a position in time and space would seem capable of having these traits. Being an intelligent man, Plato surely saw that his Forms couldn't always be self predicating. Reasoning in this manner, many of his commentators have concluded either that Plato's descriptions of the Forms cannot be taken at face value or that, realizing the error of his youthful ways, he eventually abandoned his theory of the Forms entirely.

The textual evidence that Plato ever doubted or withdrew his principle that the Forms are self predicating is, by virtually universal admission, scarce. Accordingly, the task of his would-be defenders has been very difficult. One desperate effort has even been made to reconcile Plato's text with his intelligence by arguing that he wasn't perceptive enough to note a simple ambiguity of Greek grammar—an ambiguity that hid from him the senselessness of ascribing to his Forms the properties they are the Forms for.[3] The desperate nature of such an effort suggests that caution is in order when one is tempted not to take Plato's text at face value. The one prime bit of evidence that he did consciously doubt the principle of self predication occurs in the *Parmenides* in the form of the so-called Third Man argument. Because this argument can be read as a criticism by Plato himself of his theory of the Forms, it has been seized upon as proof that he was aware, however imperfectly, of the absurdity of attributing to all Forms the properties they are the Forms for. The argument is given by Parmenides in response to an admission by Socrates—who is presented as a very young man just beginning his career—that when a number of things seem large to him he supposes that a common, single character unites them and that largeness is therefore a single thing (132 A). Parmenides replies that if many apparently large things are large by virtue of this one character, namely the Form The Large Itself, and if the Form is also large, then largeness cannot be a single thing after all. A second Form must be postulated to account for The Large Itself and other large things being large. Thus Parmenides generates an embar-

3. G. Vlastos, "The Unity of the Virtues in the *Protagoras*," *Review of Metaphysics* 25 (1972): 415-58.

rassing regress of Forms from the joint membership of Forms and particulars in a class.

Some commentators have thought Parmenides' argument to be a decisive and honest objection to the theory of the Forms, citing as the basic factor the impossibility Plato faces of ever allowing his Forms to be anything but self predicating.[4] Other commentators have pronounced the argument faulty, holding that Plato faces no such impossibility and that, in fact, he always refers to Forms and particulars in ways that prohibit their being classed together.[5] Still others have combined elements of these views, claiming that after he considered the force of Parmenides' argument, Plato felt obliged late in life to give up his theory of the Forms or, at least, to stop writing of them as self predicating.[6] In all these cases the Third Man is judged as showing that a Platonic Form cannot have, without disastrous paradox or serious qualification, the property it is the Form for.

There is ample reason to reject all these positions and the judgment they share. The Forms are always self predicating, and the Third Man poses no challenge to that essential feature of Plato's system. It challenges, rather, Socrates'

4. Two writers taking this general line are W. G. Runciman, "Plato's *Parmenides*," in *Studies in Plato's Metaphysics*, ed. R. E. Allen (London: Routledge and Kegan Paul, 1965), and R. A. Shiner, "Self-Predication and the 'Third Man' Argument," *Journal of the History of Philosophy* 8 (1970): 371-86.

5. Many writers have taken this line, including R. E. Allen, "Participation and Predication in Plato's Middle Dialogues," in *Studies in Plato's Metaphysics*, ed. R. E. Allen (London: Routledge and Kegan Paul, 1965), P. T. Geach, "The Third Man Again," in *Studies in Plato's Metaphysics*, ed. R. E. Allen, A. L. Peck, "Plato versus Parmenides," *The Philosophical Review* 71 (1962): 159-84, J. M. E. Moravscik, "The 'Third Man' Argument and Plato's Theory of Forms," *Phronesis* 8 (1963): 50-62, H. E. Cherniss, "The Relation of the *Timaeus* to Plato's Later Dialogues," in *Studies in Plato's Metaphysics*, ed. R. E. Allen, G. Vlastos, "Postscript to the Third Man: A Reply to Mr. Geach," in *Studies in Plato's Metaphysics*, ed. R. E. Allen, and S. Peterson, "A Reasonable Self-Predication Premise for the Third Man Argument," *The Philosophical Review* 82 (1973): 451-70.

6. Two examples of writers with this view of Plato are K. W. Rankin, "The Duplicity of Plato's Third Man," *Mind* 78 (1969): 178-97, and G. Ryle, *Plato's Progress* (Cambridge: Cambridge University Press, 1966).

youthful assumption that class terms, such as *large* and *equal*, really apply to particulars. How can, Parmenides' point is, the argument that largeness is a single thing rest on the admission that many things are large? His question is met by acknowledging its cogency. At the end of his life in the *Phaedo* Socrates is careful to deny that the more or less equal things we call equal really are what we say they are. They are only apparently equal. Likewise, particulars are only apparently large, or red, or moving, or whatever else we say they are. If they really deserved the predicates we apply to them, they would cease to be bits of appearance and become realities. There is only one thing that is truly equal, Equality Itself, and only one thing that is truly large, Largeness Itself. Thus a distinction central to Plato's metaphysics between a unitary reality and a plurality of appearances saves the principle that a Form is a single thing. The warning implicit in the Third Man is that we cannot make language applicable to a world of apparent motion and multiplicity while preserving its power to express what is true. It is, one would think, obvious that Plato took that warning seriously. The Third Man is not a reproach to his beliefs; it is their basis. Virtually the whole of his dualistic epistemology and metaphysics is a response to Parmenides' argument.

To see more clearly that the Third Man is not a challenge to the principle that a Form has the property it is the Form for, it will be helpful to examine some efforts made by commentators friendly to Plato to deny or limit that principle. These are efforts invariably made in behalf of Plato's intelligence. They are efforts, however, that succeed in doing little justice to that obvious enough facet of his personality, for they reduce his system to a shambles.

The passage 158 A in the *Parmenides* reads that "What participates in The One must be other than one, since otherwise it wouldn't *participate* but would *be* one, whereas only The One can *be* one." Taking "participates in" as coextensive with "has," Cherniss argues that this and similar passages show being x and having x to be quite distinct for Plato. In that case there is no self predication of the Forms. The One and The Large are The One and The Large, but they do not have either unity or the dimensions of a large thing. The "is" of identity in Cherniss's view is distinct from the "is" of predication, and the Forms are only to be identified, not described.

In assessing Cherniss's thesis it is well to bear in mind that Plato might be claiming that anything participating in a Form does not have the property of that Form. What participates in The One is other than one, and that may mean the participant lacks unity. "Participation" may be a relation preventing a thing from being a member of a class, not the relation that makes it a member by giving it features that would justify the use of a class term. It is possible, in short, to understand Plato in a way opposite to Cherniss's. Having a property and participating in a Form may be incompatible, not coextensive.

Plato's metaphysics lends credence to this alternate view of participation. When he writes of the defective imagery of the world, he writes of it as participating in the Forms. But a defective image may lack the properties that make its model a member of some class. In the *Phaedo* more or less equal images participate in equality, yet the doctrine of that dialogue is that they are only apparently equal. In the *Laws* (721 C) Plato's spokesman describes men as participating in immortality through procreation. But contributing to the survival of the species does not make one immortal in Plato's view. To show that being x and having x must, nonetheless, be different, Cherniss quotes a passage in the *Republic* (597 C) where it is said that there could not be two ideal couches. If there were two, another couch would appear, the form of which the other two would possess, "and that would be the couch that really is." The *Republic*'s argument does not show that being x and having x—being The Couch and having the properties of a couch—are incompatible, for the phrase *and that would be the couch that really is* can most naturally be taken as referring to the third couch, not to the "form" the other two possess. Plato's clear intent here is to establish only the point that Forms are unities, not that their participants have what they lack. Thus Plato's text neither requires nor warrants Cherniss's thesis. Far from a Form's being x but not having x, it is far more plausible to say that for Plato if anything truly has x it is x. The *is* of predication just is for Plato the *is* of identity.

Less strenuous, but equally implausible, moves have been made by others to limit the force of Plato's attachment to the principle that Forms have the properties they are the Forms for. Several commentators have argued that for Plato language is ambiguous, the sense of a word differing as it is applied to a particular and to a Form. The Large, they agree, is large, but not in the way a particular is large. Thus the Form is without the feature that unites empirical entities into the class of empirically large things. I will examine two of these moves by way of illustrating the general point that language for Plato is not ontologically ambiguous. A word has but one meaning, and its referent is a Form that has the property it is the Form for.

Geach, Allen, and Vlastos have argued that the Forms act as standards, their contrast with particulars thereby being akin to the contrast of the standard pound to plain pounds. The point of comparing a Form to a standard is that one cannot refer in quite the same sense to *the* pound as one can to *a* pound. *Pound*, Geach claims, applies to each only analogously. If Forms are standards, they are not self predicating in any uncomfortable way. A sense that applies to a

Form does not apply to a particular, and so a common classification of appearance with reality is avoided.

Although Geach's effort to help Plato out has the merit of explaining how we might use a word in different ways when talking of Forms and particulars, it is still an effort with a number of radical faults. First, his views conflict with the doctrines of the *Phaedo*. There Plato does not write that something empirical is an equal thing while something intelligible is the equal thing. He writes that nothing empirical is an example of equality. If talking of standards, he would say that there are no empirical pounds or meters. What we call a pound isn't a real pound; it is only an apparent pound. Thus the phrase *a pound* does not truly apply to a particular. If it did, that would make the particular a real pound, and Plato's description of the world as a realm of appearance would fail. In terms of the argument of the *Phaedo*, if anything succeeds in being a pound or an equal thing, it is The Pound or The Equal. The appeal to a difference in the use of articles fails as much as the appeal to a difference in the *is* of predication and the *is* of identity to describe Plato's doctrine.

Second, taking a Form to be a standard does violence to a pervasive feature of Plato's thought on the status of the Forms. A Form is a piece of *physis*, or Nature, and is in no sense anything conventional. A standard, however, is made a standard by a purely arbitrary, conventional choice. As Geach remarks, it does not matter how much the standard pound weighs, for it is the standard pound by virtue of a convention, not by virtue of its own properties. It does not matter which of several weights is picked as the standard pound, and the one that is picked may be replaced at a later date. Standard time zones and standard units of length are also matters of convention that can, and do, change from time to time and place to place. Given Plato's concern that his Forms should be understood as unchangeable things unaffected by stipulation and convention, it is unlikely he ever thought of them as akin to standard units. That would compromise practically everything he argues for in the *Cratylus* on how language is related to its referents.

Third, Forms have epistemological and metaphysical functions that standards do not. A Form supplies meaning to a unit of speech, and so it is only by recollecting a Form that we are able to use a word and recognize what we apply it to. We can, by way of a heuristic example, identify a pictorial facsimile of Simmias only by first having seen Simmias (*Phaedo* 73 E.). A standard, however, has no such importance, and it does not illustrate Plato's doctrine of recollection. We do not need to have seen the standard meter stick to understand what a meter is. We generally will have mastered such concepts as those of *pound* and *meter* before, not after, it is decided upon what will serve as precise standards for their application. For Plato knowledge of the Forms is an absolute precondition for being able either to talk or to think; if Forms were standards, his view would be left unclear. To bolster his case, Geach calls attention to the tradition of saying that God, as something of a moral standard, is just and wise in a way superior to the notions of justice and wisdom we have about men; but that tradition cannot be traced to Plato as Geach believes it could. The theologian is likely to say that we cannot understand a transcendent God in terms we use for ourselves; but Plato's point is that a transcendent Form is really all we can understand, and something we must have known to be able to talk at all. For him the world is what we cannot fully comprehend.

Aside from these epistemological deficiencies, standards do not support the existence of other things. A block of wood weighing a pound does not owe its existence to the standard pound. Yet Forms support the existence of the imagelike particulars participating in them. In the strained effort to avoid self predication of the Forms, their basic functions and status in Plato's system have been ignored.

Vlastos and Peterson have also suggested that Plato—without, Vlastos surmises, being aware of what he was doing—makes use of a so-called Pauline ambiguity in his descriptions of Forms and particulars. The word *just*, for example, could be analyzed as having two ontologically different extensions with appropriately different uses. The particular acts that participate in The Just Itself could provide one extension, the Form itself providing the other. In this fashion, they argue, we could distinguish between the ways in which temporal acts are just and the eternal Form is just. The temporal acts are just by virtue of their participation in the Form; the Form itself is just solely by causing its participants to be just. Thus we might "reinterpret" Plato to mean by *Justice Itself is just*, not that justice characterizes The Just, but only that things participating in Justice are just. This "reinterpretation" would save Plato from the absurdity of holding that his Forms actually have properties their transcendent status prevents them from having.

Two observations should suffice to show that Plato makes no use of "Pauline" predications. First, if Justice Itself is just solely because of its ability to make its participants just, no Platonic answer is forthcoming to the question of how the Form acquires its causal powers. Plato certainly attributes to his Forms the power to affect, even to bring into existence, the particulars participating in them. He explains that power, however, by comparing a Form to a model which, with the help of a light source, casts its own shadow or image onto some reflecting surface. Thus a Form affects its participants by bestowing on them a version of its own property. The Just and The Beautiful give to the world of appearance a degree of justice and beauty only because they themselves are just and beautiful. For this reason The Just could not be just solely because it makes its participants just. To make them just to any degree, it has to be just itself. The causal power of a Form requires, in short, that it be described in something other than "Pauline" terms. Vlastos's and Peterson's suggestions that a Form produces, without having, the property it gives to its participants simply conflicts with Plato's explanation of how reality affects appearance.

Second, contrary to their analysis, The Just does not make its participants really or truly just. The properties of the Forms are only weakly reflected in the world (*Phaedrus* 247 D-E). Nothing empirical fully merits the descriptions we use, and that is because the Forms do not make their participants full members of the classes language recognizes. There is, then, a clear limit to the causal power of the Forms; they never succeed in making their participants really equal, or just, or anything else. If they did, Plato's distinction between reality and appearance would fail. Thus, to suggest with Vlastos and Peterson that a Form is just or equal only because it makes its participants just or equal clearly will not do. The "Pauline" analysis of Plato's descriptions of his Forms grants to them a causal power exceeding that which Plato can allow them to have. At the same time it leaves unexplained the limited powers the Forms do have.

Other efforts have been made to establish a duality of sense for a term in applying it to particulars and to Forms, but all such efforts face impossible rigors that should now be clear. Plato thinks meaning arises from the relation between a word and the Form it refers to. Class terms, for example, are the proper names of the Forms, and it is because these terms are the names of eternal entities that they have a stable use. Thus, if a word were to have a dual sense, it would seem necessary that it name two Forms. The troublesome import of this thought is that after learning to refer to a given Form by beholding it, a second Form would have to be beheld to acquire the ability to refer to the particulars participating in the first Form. But now the regress of the Third Man is only generated anew, and it would be unclear how the sense acquired from the second Form would allow us to do anything but refer to the second Form. As long as meaning is a name relation between word and Form, only Forms can be the true subjects of speech.

Plato clearly takes the view that words name only the Forms, for he denies that we can make any intelligible statement—a *logos*—about particulars (*Timaeus* 29 A-B). The world is unknowable and the soul is immortal, not because language applies to particulars in a special sense, but because it applies only approximately. If language did apply in one sense to reality and in another sense to appearance, it should be possible for a word in its second sense to refer exactly to a particular. In that case knowledge of appearance should be possible, for an exact empirical reference would guarantee the truth of a predication. It should be possible, too, for us to use an empirical language without a prior knowledge of the Forms. To say that particulars have class traits and that language does apply to appearance is to undermine Plato's arguments for the impossibility of empirical knowledge and for the immortality of the soul. Vlastos claims that there is nothing in Plato's naive logical vocabulary that would allow him to say with any clarity that particulars are not to be joined with Forms in the same set. In a way that is true, if judged in terms of Plato's theory of language, but Plato is not naive. His point is that when talking of the world we cannot help misgrouping particulars with Forms. We have but one language; its only subjects are the Forms; thus we have no option but to apply class predicates where they do not apply if we choose to talk of empirical matters.

All efforts to avoid self predication of the Forms conflict with too many central and unsurrendered doctrines of Plato to be plausible. They undermine not merely the Third Man, but virtually the whole of Plato's system. They are in intent friendly, but in effect damaging efforts, arising not from what Plato says, but from a desire to help him escape the Third Man. Since he has his own way of doing that, they are efforts best abandoned. The Forms are fully self predicating in the one and only sense of the names they bear.

It is important to note that the denial of truth to an empirical judgment is a sufficient defense against the Third Man. It prevents the classification of Forms with the particulars participating in them. Plato's commentators, however, have long feared that if the Forms are similar in any respect to particulars, they must be classed together. Yet it is neither a truth of life nor a thesis of Plato that similar things are the same things. A defective swatch of reddish cloth is similar to a swatch of red cloth, but that does not make it red. If we lacked the concept *reddish*, we might call the reddish swatch red, and that is Plato's view of how we speak of all particulars. By recollecting something merely similar to what we see we enable ourselves to talk about the world—although only in an inexact way. Thus the similarity between Forms and particulars explains our ability to talk about particulars; it does not make our talk accurate. It is only an ignorant, dreamlike state of mind, Plato remarks, which mistakes resemblance for identity (*Republic* 476 C). He thus insists on the obvious truth that the similar are not always the same. With that insistence he undermines any need to admit that particulars belong in the classes Forms occupy. His point is applicable to all class relations. The reddish thing that fails to be red fails by the same margin to be a genuinely colored thing; the empirical drawing that fails to be a true triangle fails to belong to the genus of geometric figures. Before one can be an animal one must, so Plato's view seems to be, first have membership in the classes of flesh, fish, or fowl. Particulars always fall short of having specific traits; thus all words fall short of describing them accurately.

The Resolution of the Problem of How Empirical Terms Have Meaning

A defense of the thesis that a Form is always to be understood as having the property it is the Form for wouldn't be complete unless it dealt with the motives of those who, in the face of admittedly severe textual difficulties, have denied the principle of self predication. Neither would a major ambition of this chapter be realized. Thus the question must be faced of how Plato, obviously an intelligent man, could think that all words and all concepts apply, never to empirical objects, but always to timeless and spaceless Forms. The two crucial cases of the words *motion* and *time* may serve as the basis of a discussion. These words appear to apply to what Plato calls appearance. They must, however, apply to Forms. How, then, can *Motion Itself moves* and *Time Itself is temporal* be understood?

Vlastos and others have held that the acceptance of these propositions would shatter the coherence of Plato's theory. That is certainly an understandable judgment, but it is also a hasty one that does not take sufficiently to heart Plato's rejection of all empirical views of knowledge and meaning. Everything empirical, Plato insists, is to be identified by reference to intelligible Forms. Thus it isn't merely triangles and tangents that we identify through recollection; time and motion are to be identified in the same way. These aspects of the world are, as much as all others are, matters of appearance to which our words apply only approximately. To say, then, that an animal moves is as untrue as to say that some figure is a triangle. What we call motion or time isn't real motion or real time. They are mere images, or imperfect versions, of what we say they are. Given Plato's views on language, the words *motion* and *time* must, like all other words, refer to perfectly static, eternal Forms. When these entities are referred to, they must mean virtually the opposite of what the naive think they mean, for they cannot refer without applying; and if they apply to the static and the eternal, then they have a meaning opposed to empirical presumptions. What we mistakenly call time is actually an image of eternity (*Timaeus* 37 D-E). What we mistakenly call motion is actually, Plato appears to hold also, an image of rest (*Timaeus* 30 A-B). *Motion* and *rest* as well as *time* and *eternity* would therefore seem to be, in spite of usage to the contrary, synonyms.

That *time* and *eternity* have the same meaning may appear to be an extravagant form of cooperation with Plato's text. There are, however, strong reasons for thinking otherwise. As a teleologist, Plato believed that the world is goal directed. The whole of appearance, he held, is a living work of art that is at least partially governed by a desire to be as like reality as possible. Appearance strives to be like the Forms (*Phaedo* 75 A-D). What we normally call change is, paradoxically, an aspect of a partially unsuccessful effort to be unchanging. The stars, for example, are obliged to move, as we say, in space, but there is a sense in which they really do not want to go anywhere. Thus they revolve back to their positions every day, thereby making themselves as stable and unchanging as their imperfect status allows them to be (*Timaeus* 30 A-B). Substellar, mortal organisms cannot manage to move so uniformly as the stars, but they, too, share in the teleology of the heavens by striving to be perfect, unchanging, and immortal. Reproduction, through which a species lasts forever, is one means they use to seek their end. Thus the goal of every changing thing is to be unchanging. Rest, not motion, is the natural state of all things—a firm principle of Platonic physics that was not reversed until the time of Galileo.

If, as Plato argues, what we call time and motion is organized to give the world as many features of an unchanging reality as possible, then what we call motion and time can be compared to a defective image of some intelligible pattern that that image reflects. Since, too, all images are to be identified by reference to what they are images of, we can say that the names we apply to this particular image are really the names of the pattern it reflects and that—as with all other empirical habits of speech—only by courtesy do we call it what we do. Time, so called, is the image of eternity. Since the names of the Forms are the names we use when talking of empirical matters, we must conclude that, when understood, *time* and *eternity* are synonyms. The same is true of *motion* and *rest*. Plato translates words that he thinks can make no sense as used, into synonyms of words that do make sense.

The partially incoherent world of empirical experience acquires a degree of intelligibility for Plato only because what we call the element of change within it is actually a defective version of what is truly intelligible: changeless being. What we call change is related to changeless being in the very way the approximately equal sticks of the *Phaedo* are related to true Equality. What we call change is only apparent change. Since the goal of all appearance is to be a real version of itself, change—so called—is part of an effort to become real change. Thus real change and rest are the same, for rest is also the goal and natural state of everything that appears to move in space. If things in the world were ever to become truly, not just apparently, changeable, they would cease to do what we say they do when, in our confused mode of talk, we say they change. An echo of Plato's doctrine can be heard in Aristotle. Rectilinear motion in the substellar regions of the world, he writes, is an imitation of the more nearly perfect, circular motion of the stars (*On Generation and Corruption* 337a 4). The heavens themselves rotate so as to be like the perfect, immobile, timeless activity of the prime mover (*Metaphysics* 12. 7). Since stellar rotation is an image or picture of an activity that must serve to identify the derivative image itself, the true referent of the word *rotation* must be the prime mover's motionless activity. That, at any rate, is the way Plato would put the matter. For him *motion* and *time* really apply to something like the activity of Aristotle's prime mover. What we, in our empirical concerns, call time and motion are but defective versions of the Truly Moving and the Truly Temporal—that is, immobile, eternal being. Thus for Plato there is nothing philosophically grotesque about saying "Motion Itself moves" and "Time Itself is temporal." That amounts to saying that the Forms Motion and Time are immobile and eternal.

There is, to be sure, a difficulty in Plato's doctrine for the philosophically unsophisticated who have not seen how shot through with confusion and incoherence ordinary usage is of words such as *motion* and *time*. The cure for that difficulty cannot lie, however, in accepting the opinions reason has indicted. It must lie in learning the true meaning of words apart from their usage. Plato did not accept standard Greek as providing a coherent basis for deciding the meaning of words and sentences. Most men, he held, are like ignorant prisoners in a cave without knowledge of the true sense of what they say and think. They need to be shown that the actual reference of everything they say lies beyond their cavernous world. Plato did not try to match his language with what he took to be the confused talk of those who saw no problem in saying "Change is real." It is more than likely that no one will ever find what so many commentators have looked for: some facet of Greek usage that would make Plato's description of his Forms sound reassuringly level-headed and plausible. His indictment of men and women who think their words apply to the flickering, incoherent shadows about them when, in fact, they apply to utterly stable, fully intelligible realities elsewhere, indicates that he anticipated, even experienced, from his fellow Greeks as much puzzlement about his descriptions of the Forms as scholars treating his work have expressed. That puzzlement is not a function of a corrigible lack of philological insight into the subtleties of a language Plato was obviously a master of; it is a function of a philosophical failure to see that Plato assigned to the spatial and temporal concepts that troubled him and his predecessors a sense opposed to common sense. Although in some respects it might be fair, in others it is surely pointless to hold to our standards of clarity and coherence an educator who would initiate us into the paradoxical knowledge that many of the terms we believe to be contrasting are, in fact, equivalent. The very search for a linguistically reasonable "reinterpretation" of Plato's descriptions of his Forms is, in Platonic terms, a muddle.

Plato's Final Reply to Parmenides: The Priority of Thought over Sensation

The translation of words like *motion* and *time* into words like *rest* and *eternity* is, of course, not merely a device to save the principle of self predication. It is also Plato's final answer to Parmenides and Zeno. He agreed with them that there is something unintelligible about change, and so something amiss with our use of words denoting it. Rather than declare those words incoherent, however, he argued that they mean something different from what they seem to mean and refer, in truth, to what is intelligible. Being always identifies what becomes; Nature is always the referent of art. It is with this argument that Plato undermines Parmenides' extreme, invidious duality between intelligible and empirical science. The words and concepts necessary to a description of the world are coherent. They do not, of course, apply in full to the world, and thus an empirical science is imperfect in the sense that its results cannot be known to be true. Still, what we say when talking about a moving, temporal world is intelligible, not nonsensical; and the proximity of what we say to the truth allows us to have right opinions, not total falsehoods, about empirical matters. What, in short, Parmenides declared to be unintelligible, illusory phenomena is for Plato a defective version of the intelligible and real. The ultimate reason why appearance has a standing higher than sheer illusion is that such trustworthy, intelligible concepts as *rest* and *eternity* lend their meaning to such suspect, empirical concepts as *motion* and *time*. We may not realize that many of our words are synonyms, of course, and so the price paid for a defense of empirical inquiry is the indictment of common opinions on the meaning of language as suffering from cavernous ignorance and giddy confusion. Meaning for Plato is divorced from usage. Consequently, we don't always realize the import of what we say, any more than we always realize what it is that our words refer to.

There are, too, other prices Plato pays for his stand. He is immediately obliged to indict as partly irrational the erotic instincts responsible for what we call change and reproduction. He succeeds, however, in buying the means he needs to defend, not just empirical inquiry, but art and culture. I now want to take up these matters by examining the consequences for biological and psychological theory that Plato draws from his reply to Parmenides.

3

Psychology–The Contest between the Human and the Divine

The Paradoxical Teleology of Appearance and the World's Disorderly Motion

When Plato identifies everything timely and spatial in terms of the eternal and spaceless, the paradoxical conclusions he comes to on the meaning of empirical descriptions align themselves with equally paradoxical conclusions about the aims of the organic instincts. He claims that the cosmos is a living animal. It is besouled, and all its parts respond to an organic teleology. In its purest, most rational form that teleology consists of the effort of living appearances to maintain and to improve themselves so as to be as similar as possible to the eternal realities they participate in (*Phaedo* 75 A-B). Sensible and relative things strive after the intelligible and absolute qualities they imperfectly reflect. Art, in other words, aspires to the status of Nature. Particulars try to be genuine, real instances of what they merely apparently are, and they try to be that in some static way. Thus the movements begun by soul take place for the sake of turning ephemeral particulars into closer likenesses of the stable Forms. That paradox is as fundamental to Plato's biological and psychological theory as it is to his metaphysics and his theory of knowledge.

It is easy to note the paradoxical core of the teleology Plato sees in appearance. If mortal organisms move, change, and reproduce in order to partake of immortality and to be like an utterly static pattern in other respects, they use means that doom their effort to failure. The prime condition of static rest can never be met. What we call motion may be a botched version of rest, but to engage continuously in what we call motion is still to guarantee that we never will enjoy a true, full rest. Our means, no matter how described, are fundamentally incapable of bringing us to our goal. This truth amounts to Plato's guarantee that appearance will never be the same as reality. Like Zeno's arrows and racers, living things can only approach, and never gain, their end.

The hopeless nature of life's ambitions suggests that there is a link between Plato's teleology and what the *Timaeus* (30A) refers to as a disorderly motion in "the whole visible sphere" of the world, which the *demiourgos* combats so as to make creation as nearly perfect as he can. When the *demiourgos* improves on the preexistent art work of the world sphere, focusing its imagery so as to picture reality more clearly, he gets it to forgo as far as is possible the use of motion as a means of portraying the Forms. Of seven possible motions, for example, six were taken from the visible animal that is the world, leaving it to revolve on its axis without deviation (*Timaeus* 34 A). In working to eliminate disorderly motion, the *demiourgos* is trying to promote appearance's true teleology. He brings the moving stars closer to their goal of immobile reality. Appearance must move in any effort to gain its end, for if it didn't move at all it would fail to incorporate into itself any element of an abiding, stable life. An animal that failed to reproduce, for example, would partake not at all of immortality (*Symposium* 208 A). It would simply appear, then disappear with no ties to an eternal life. Still, any motion precludes full success. Thus the world is only as rational as it might be when it moves with the greatest possible economy. If things have to change to be like an unchanging reality, then it is well and reasonable that they change no more than they have to. So it is that the *demiourgos* acts to guarantee a rational economy of effort in the celestial regions of the cosmos. He limits motion in order that appearance might better approach the unattainable goal of being a static, conceptually perfect reality. He reminds the world, so to speak, that the end and model of all movement is something eternally at rest, and that to move excessively is therefore to conflict with the reason for moving. He fails, of course, to realize his ambition fully. He does not deprive the stars of all motion and does not, therefore, make the heavens exactly like the Nature of the Forms. He merely brings to fulfillment as far as is possible the teleology implicit in the art work of appearance.

The functions Plato assigns to the *demiourgos* would indicate that the disorderly motion he combats arises from the paradoxical teleology of motion itself. The instincts responsible for organic change appear to become irrationally committed to change as a proximate end when faced with the paradoxical task of giving, through change, the marks of reality, or Nature, to appearance, or art. In order to see the point of this observation, it is necessary to consider an implicit but far-reaching contrast Plato draws between man's building activity and his erotic, reproductive efforts. The first is intelligent and orderly in ways the second is not. These two activities would thus seem to be related in a way similar to the way the orderly work of the *demiourgos* is related to the excessive, disorderly movements he eliminates from the heavens.

A Contrast between Industrial and Organic Processes

In the *Philebus* (54 A-C) Socrates claims that becoming always takes place for the sake of being. His point is that a process has a distinct goal—that means are used to achieve an end beyond themselves. Shipbuilding, for example, goes on for the sake of ships, rather than ships being for the sake of shipbuilding. In this and all similar cases certain features basic to an intelligent process are present. The shipbuilder, desiring a ship, uses means that allow him to build a complete ship; he picks means appropriate to his task. His building activity is also for the sake of something other than itself; his primary aim is to have a ship. Thus the terminal of his work and the goal of his work coincide; as soon as he has the ship he wants, he stops building. Then, too, he invents; he makes something he needs and does not already have; he works in anticipation of a novel satisfaction.

When one examines Plato's views on why organisms change, move, and reproduce, it is clear that what he regards as the features of intelligent design are missing in what we call nature. Nature does not work on its own like a reasonable craftsman. When, for example, the stars are said to rotate and plants and animals are said to reproduce so as to participate as best they can in the eternal properties of an unchanging reality, a clearly inappropriate means is used. No other means may be available, but it is still a means that will never produce the desired effect. Nothing can ever become fully like a static model by moving. Yet that is precisely what organic nature sets out to do.

The inappropriateness of the means open to living things for the gaining of their prime end appears to be responsible for other, more telling differences between organic and industrial processes. Unable to be utterly immortal and unchanging, the stars and all other empirical things set themselves to achieving a secondary, possible goal. In lieu of an eternal rest they do not have and can never experience, the stars simply try to move forever; in lieu of a genuine immortality for themselves, plants and animals try to guarantee the continuity of their species by reproducing. They come to long, not for the being of the Forms themselves, but for the continuous becoming of conception and generation that merely pictures the Forms—or so claims Diotima in the *Symposium* (206 D-E). The bodily organs, too, continually deplete themselves so as to gain in cyclic replenishments such pleasures as those which accompany eating and drinking (*Philebus* 32 A).

Now, however, means and end, activity and product, coincide. Endless motion is what the stars seek, and that is what they gain by moving endlessly. Perpetual replenishment of the species is what an animal seeks, and that is what it helps to guarantee by reproducing itself. Pleasure, too, is what a bodily organ pursues, but pleasure itself is just a process (*Philebus* 53 C). Thus pleasure is what the organism experiences through a movement from depletion to satiety. The process undergone is no longer for the sake of something distinct from itself. Appearances move out of an infatuation with motion, propagation, and pleasure for their own endless sake, not out of a desire to have the features of a static reality. As a result, the world's art does not come so close as it might to having the features of Nature. The inevitable frustration of organic processes seems to insure that those processes turn into the world's proximate goals. Organic nature is like a shipbuilder who clumsily builds forever as the next best thing to having the complete and perfect ship that always eludes him.

When means and end come to coincide, the terminal and goal of an activity are, of course, sundered. The reason is that the goal of the activity is to have no terminal. There is no way the stars could ever stop moving and also attain their proximate goal, for what they seek in lieu of eternal rest is endless motion. Likewise, there is no way the goal of specific continuity could be achieved without an endless, cyclical series of births. The instinctual pursuit of pleasure, too, would not be attained without a cyclical change in an organism, for pleasure just is a process of replenishment akin to that of eating and drinking. Perpetual change is essential to the proximate goals organic nature is capable of attaining, whether those goals be pleasure, vicarious immortality, or a life of the stars equivalent to time itself. Thus one might say that, unlike industrial design, nature is ruled at a proximate level by a telos-less teleology. Its end, in the sense of a goal, is never to have an end, in the sense of a terminal. The natural state of things, rest, ceases to be the telos of change, just as does the gaining of some class-determining trait that for Plato only a thing at rest ever truly has. Defective particulars reproduce their own kind only to enable their own kind to go on reproducing. One reason nature merely duplicates itself in this fashion is that all organic desires are fixed by memory of past satisfactions (*Philebus* 35 E). When in a state of tension and depletion, an animal will remember what relieved its distress before. It will then repeat some past action, such as eating, forgetting all aims but those stored in the memory. For Plato the whole of organic nature moves in a similar way. The result is that nature is a conservative realm, moving, not in anticipation of a novel satisfaction, but in longing for what it has already felt. It is, then, a realm that neither adds to nor improves upon itself. It remains, and must remain so long as the organic instincts are left unchecked, the incomplete, botched art the *Timaeus, Republic, Statesman, Sophist*, and *Phaedrus* describe it as being.

The contrasts between the intelligent art of the industrial artisan and the unintelligent art of nature would seem to provide the reasons why the world sphere requires the rational supervision of the *demiourgos* to avoid a disorderly, excessive motion. In excluding the vision of a terminal being from its goals, living nature is prone merely to reproduce itself and to move more than is either necessary or of use for the clearest picturing of reality. Plato is careful to separate his intelligent *demiourgos* from nature's defective teleology; that figure leaves to the endlessly rotating stars control of the substellar, erotic, and reproductive processes of plant and animal life (*Timaeus* 41 C-D). His function would seem to be that of making as sure as he can that the ultimate aims of appearance to be like a static reality are not unduly thwarted in the world's celestial regions by the desire of living things to duplicate the past forever. His hope is that his work will inspire man to right the vagaries of his own earthly life. The limits he places on the motion of the world sphere would seem to be his way of showing that beyond the self-contained aims of ceaseless change lies the ultimate, if unattainable, prize of eternal perfection and rest, wherein the goal and terminal of motion would coincide. The speech of Socrates in the *Symposium* (200 D-201 B) would seem to make the same theoretical point, for there he insists that the movements of love and desire are not for the sake of what is or has been, but for the sake of a beauty that is not yet to hand.

There is need to stress that the hope of the *demiourgos* is the hope that man will act as the *demiourgos* himself does. It is not, as Callahan claims,[1] the hope that man will imitate the

1. J. F. Callahan, *Four Views of Time in Ancient Philosophy* (Cambridge, Mass.: Harvard University Press, 1948), p. 28.

stars. If he were to do that, he would act like all other plants and animals and move endlessly, with endless motion as his only goal. Plato's injunction is that man should not take anything empirical, such as the heavens, for a guide to live by, but the intelligible Forms. He should, by recollecting the Forms, give the same kind of order to his life that the *demiourgos* has given to the stars. He cannot do that by imitating the stars directly. He has to see and long for what the stars themselves are ultimately trying to do and be like. Imitating an empirical model will never correct the disorderly movements within us. The immortal reason of man can have no concern with the moving image we call time except as a heuristic indicator of what it pictures. Thus it is surely a mistake to think that for Plato right and rational conduct consists of imitating the stars. That kind of conduct is precisely what is wrong with the substellar world. It is conduct that leaves appearance incomplete and botched.

The work of the *demiourgos* is required by the failure of unaided organic nature to match as closely as it might the features of intelligent design. It is because living things, unlike shipwrights, tend to equate means with ends and divorce goals from terminals that the *demiourgos* intervenes in the world's celestial regions to bring order out of disorder. Because his intervention takes place so as to make the living heavens move more intelligently, the obvious conclusion to be drawn is that for Plato the erotic, life-sustaining teleology of the substellar world isn't fully rational. His text bears out that conclusion.[2] The life-sustaining impulses we

2. A further reason for inferring that Plato thinks the organic instincts are irrational is that Aristotle, possibly echoing his teacher, believes they are. An intelligent action is for the sake of an end, he writes, wherein all preceding steps are taken to bring a series to a completion (*Physics* 199a 7-13). His point is that a rational goal will coincide with the state of rest that is natural to all things. Given this mark of intelligence, the effort of the organic instincts to perpetuate life forever is obviously irrational. This is, of course, a familiar view of instinctual activity. Freud, for example, contrasts instinctual to intelligent effort on the grounds that Plato and Aristotle use. He writes that living organisms, dominated by a life instinct, struggle energetically against events that would help them attain

feel to eat, drink, and reproduce are irrational (*Republic* 439 D). A true philosopher, committed to a rational teleology, would not concern himself with the pleasures associated with these impulses (*Phaedo* 64 D; *Republic* 607 A; *Philebus* 33 B). The indictment by Parmenides and Zeno of change thus has as its heritage in Plato the indictment of the instincts responsible for change. They fall short of intelligence in the way that change itself, with only further change as its goal, falls short of coherence.

Alternate Explanations of the World's Disorderly Motion

Plato's commentators have long wondered about the origin of the disorderly motion mentioned in the *Timaeus*. Soul, says Plato, starts all movement, but the *demiourgos*, so he also says, uses intelligence and soul to combat a primal disorder. What, then, is the source of that disorder? Rather than locate it in the paradoxical character of the teleology of motion itself, many of Plato's interpreters have made alternate suggestions, which require attention. Since the *Phaedrus* (245 E) and the *Laws* (892 A) unequivocally trace the origin of motion to soul, Cornford[3] and Morrow[4] have held that a rational soul, the *demiourgos*, is responsible for orderly motion and that an irrational part of the world's soul is responsible for disorderly motion. One trouble with their thesis is that Plato does not mention a specifically irrational

their true, thanatological ends rapidly. Such behavior is characteristic of instinctive as contrasted to intelligent effort (S. Freud, *Beyond the Pleasure Principle* (New York: Bantam Books, 1959), p. 72). It may also be noted that Freud associates the irrationality of the life instincts with what he calls a compulsion to repeat the past—a compulsion arising from the desire of an organism to reexperience some past satisfaction. The consequences for psychological theory of Plato's reply to the paradoxes of Parmenides and Zeno are far from dead.

3. F. M. Cornford, *Plato's Cosmology*, p. 205.

4. G. R. Morrow, "Necessity and Persuasion in Plato's *Timaeus*," in *Studies in Plato's Metaphysics*, ed. R. E. Allen (London: Routledge and Kegan Paul, 1965).

part of the world's soul. As a counterthesis, Vlastos[5] has maintained that in spite of doctrinal claims to the contrary, not all motion, but only teleologically directed motion, can be traced to the initiative of soul. The soul's motion supervenes on, without causing, undirected, disorderly motion of a purely mechanical origin. Crombie has argued for much the same thesis.[6]

These rival views on how to understand Plato's text have a number of dubious points in common. They both distinguish between genetically different kinds of motion when, in fact, there is no textual basis for such a distinction. Just as there is no mention of a distinctively irrational part of the world's soul that could create a special kind of motion different from that of a rational soul, so there is no mention in the *Timaeus* of a self-originating mechanical motion that operates independently of soul. After finishing his account of the world's teleology, Plato does turn to a description of mechanical, or secondary, causation, wherein he mentions a "variable cause" that produces random effects "without order or design." He states, however, that this variable cause does not originate motion, but merely transmits it when compelled to do so (*Timaeus* 46 E). There is, then, no recognition by Plato of genetically different kinds of motion.

Vlastos, Crombie, Cornford, and Morrow also assume without good reason that the disorderly motion the *demiourgos* combats in the early part of the *Timaeus* is produced by the "variable cause." Plato, however, remarks that a mechanical, or transmitting, principle of causation is present in all phenomena and that intelligence "persuaded" it to guide the greater part of created things toward perfection

5. G. Vlastos, "The Disorderly Motion in the *Timaeus*," in *Studies in Plato's Metaphysics*, ed. R. E. Allen.

6. I. M. Crombie, *An Examination of Plato's Doctrines*, 2: 216-19.

(*Timaeus* 47 E-48 A). Random, mechanical effects are responsible, for example, for the winnowing of the elements of air, earth, fire, and water into regions where like is mixed with like (*Timaeus* 53 A). These purely chance, undirected, and variable effects contribute to the world's overall order. Where a bit of chaff will fall from a winnowing basket is in some measure a matter of chance. Still, the light and the heavy pieces separate into different piles. The *demiourgos* has no reason to interfere with or regret the orderly result. Random effects are thus clearly compatible with, even necessary to, an intelligently ruled world. The disorderly motion mentioned in the *Timaeus* is not. The undesigned, chance effects the variable cause produces are also always present (*Timaeus* 46 E).There is, then, no particularly good textual reason to identify them with what the *demiourgos* eliminated from the heavens when he brought order out of disorder. Apart from these difficulties, it may be mentioned that the efforts of Cornford and Morrow to tie the presence of supposedly undesirable chance effects to an irrational element in the world soul make Plato's position incoherent. If disorder is to be explained as a function of chance, it cannot also be explained as a function of design, irrational or otherwise. The claim of Vlastos and Crombie does not tax Plato with an obvious inconsistency, but it does meet headlong an equally severe problem. If, as they assume, the world's irrational disorder is of a purely mechanical nature, then the clearly stated principle that soul starts all motion has to be given up. With the surrender of that principle Plato's attack upon materialism fails, and his dialogues are abandoned to the worst kind of chaos. Even the *Timaeus* is left in disorder, for its prime thesis is that the world is a product of art and design, of foresight and choice—not of chance. Short of charging Plato with an obvious inconsistency or a dramatic, unexplained change of mind, there is simply no way that the disorder the *demiourgos* combats in the *Timaeus* can be equated with the mechanical, secondary cause of necessity.

Apart from having no textual basis and inviting a dubious equation, the distinction between genetically different kinds of motion does violence to Plato's description of the work of the *demiourgos*. Vlastos, for example, writes of some kind of coherent motion's being imposed by the *demiourgos* on unintelligent chaos when, in fact, all he does is eliminate motion. He does not add motion of any kind to anything; he subtracts it. He removes from the stars all rectilinear motion, setting them in a purely circular orbit. Thus the improvement of the world by the *demiourgos* has nothing to do with genetically different kinds of motion, one of which supervenes on the other. Disorderly motion is simply excessive motion that has, so to speak, forgotten that its true telos is rest. Plato does not distinguish between coherent and incoherent motion—only more and less motion, all of which is less than fully intelligible. The whole world of change falls short of being intelligible by virtue of its changeable nature. There is, then, no distinction whatsoever between what Vlastos calls occurrences capable of rational explanation and occurrences incapable of rational explanation.

It is important, too, to bear in mind that the partial incoherence of change is not an illusion produced in us by our finite minds, which fail to detect all the causes of change. Taylor holds that Plato's wandering cause, necessity, is only symbolic of human ignorance and that it would vanish from our account of the world if we were to have full, not partial, knowledge of appearance.[7] But there is, of course, no possibility of empirical knowledge in Plato's

7. A. E.Taylor, *A Commentary on Plato's Timaeus* (London: Oxford University Press, 1928). p. 300.

view. His position may be unpalatable to those who, like Taylor, honor the progress of science, but there is little point in trying to make him look like a modern philosopher with faith in the ultimate intelligibility of all phenomena. Whatever the psychological rewards might be in thinking that Plato shared one's faith, they cannot compensate for the effort required to support Taylor's view that Plato believed the world to be, in principle, intelligible. Motion, all of it, really is less than completely coherent. That is why empirical propositions are nothing more than likely stories and why no one, the *demiourgos* included, has knowledge of the changeable world.

Clearly it would seem best that one look for the source of the disorder the *demiourgos* combats in the paradoxical teleology of motion itself. Such a source is compatible with the point that Plato is discussing the world's teleology—not mechanics—when he mentions the disorderly motion. It is, too, a source that does not require the dubious equation of disorder with the chance effects that Plato describes as capable of contributing to the overall order of the cosmos. Likewise, it does not tax Plato with an inconsistency or an unexplained, radical change of position. It also explains why, instead of adding movement, the *demiourgos* works to insure that the heavens move with the greatest possible economy. Apart from these advantages, there is the further point to be made that man's relation to the terrestrial world is for Plato analogous to the relation of the *demiourgos* to the heavens. As already noted, one reason why the *demiourgos* corrected the motion of the stars was to give mankind a lesson in how to regulate his own vagaries, which tend to match the irregular and graceless ways of the terrestrial world in general (*Timaeus* 47 B-E). Man's improvement of himself and the world has nothing to do with combating the chance effects of mechanical causation; nor does it involve his adding either rational or purposeful motion to what already exists. It has to do with his getting things to respond on their own to the ultimate telos of appearance—to guide them toward perfection. Man's role as an animal breeder, for example, does not involve his attacking mechanical effects, his imparting a special motion to anything, or his giving a teleology to what is totally devoid of purpose. It involves, rather, his intervention—by way of stock selection—in the living, soul-directed activity of procreation so as to insure that the birth of a calf, a pup, or a child has as its end something beyond itself—that appearance moves to become like the reality it isn't. If man abandons his breeding efforts, his pedigreed cocks and hunting dogs will quickly procreate inferior versions of themselves (*Republic* 459 B). Their progeny will degenerate, and not because of purely mechanical difficulties they must face, but because all organisms become infatuated with pleasure, losing sight of the ultimate goals of appearance. This is the reason man himself, says Socrates, stands in need of a breeder (*Apology* 20 A-D). His organic instincts are far removed from philosophy, reason, law, and order (*Republic* 587 A-B). Likewise, a charioteer's correction of the disorderly movements of the horses that pull his chariot does not involve his moving the careening vehicle himself; he pulls the reins fixed to the horses, to be sure, but to restrain without adding to their motion. They then move the chariot on their own (*Phaedrus* 254 C). The role of the rational *demiourgos* is similar. He corrects a teleological, not a mechanical disorder; and he does that without having to impart any genetically distinct motion of his own to the world. He shows that the work of reason is required by the pervasive tendency of all living things to neglect the ultimate end of appearance. Plato is a teleological as well as an ontological dualist. There are, he insists, two kinds of appearances: one kind that is regulated by a rational principle of causation, and another kind that is regulated by the irrational appetites, which leave the art they make incomplete and botched.

The Contrast between the Human and the Divine

The contrast Plato draws between industrial design and organic reproduction is not merely a contrast between intelligent and unintelligent behavior. It is also a contrast between the activities of different agencies. This point may strike one as queer, for the shipwright who builds a ship would seem capable of reproducing without changing his identity. Yet, for Plato matters are not as they may appear to be. The ship a man builds is a product of human art. The child he sires, however, is an animal belonging to the organic order of nature. Since nature is really divine art, the child has to be considered the product of a divine, not human, agency. All men, in Plato's express judgment, are the offspring of divine workmanship (*Sophist* 266 B). The basic biological impulse in every mortal creature, including man, is to partake of an eternal life through reproduction (*Symposium* 208 A-B). By so partaking of the eternal, an immortal something appears in the midst of our mortality—and that something is what is divine about us (*Symposium* 206 C). The unintelligent, excessive, and conservative processes of organic nature are, then, divine. The intelligent, orderly, and novel processes of industrial design are, in contrast, human.

Just how Plato's distinction between the human and the divine is to be understood, and just how it applies to us, are questions that can be answered in full only by examining Plato's views on how we are related to nature. Before any such examination is attempted, however, it will be well to make a few preliminary points that bear on the issues already discussed and that also call attention to other contrasts Plato aligns with the distinction between the human and the divine. In linking, as he obviously does, unintelligent behavior with the divine art of nature, Plato is preparing the ground for a defense of urban culture. If industrial design is related to organic change as the intelligent is related to the unintelligent, and if the intelligent is somehow the human whereas the unintelligent is somehow the divine, then culture—being human art—stands justified before nature. Man, with his intelligent skills, is in a position to improve upon nature as well as to add to it. His position in the substellar world is similar to that of the *demiourgos* in the heavens. By bringing the restraints of intelligence to bear on the frenetic, disorderly pursuit of terrestrial becoming for its own sake, he can improve on the world's art work, turning the unnecessarily distorted images of plant and animal and even his own life into superior, clearer, less changeable, and healthier portraits of reality. He can act as a physician and breeder to nature and to himself—as an artisan who corrects the botched, unintelligent work of designers less gifted than he is. He can, of course, never make terrestrial nature perfect—no more than the *demiourgos* could perfect the heavens—for nothing merely apparent can be made a reality. Still, in spite of his inability to attain his end, he can make sure that the end remains distinct from the processes used to approach it; and in that crucial respect he can impose the prime condition of intelligent design on biological creativity. He is properly the regulator of nature's defective teleology, and that role implies that his primary loyalties should be to himself and his culture, not to the unintelligent realm he is meant to rule. A life lived in accord with nature, so called, can only be a life that is irrational and botched. We have, then, good reason to prefer culture to nature, the city to the wilderness, and rule by reason to rule by instinct.

A second point that should be made about Plato's contrast of the human to the divine follows from the observation that man can aid nature's art only because he is in a position to see and to share its true, although obscured, goals. He must be able to understand that the actual goal of all organic change is not mere repetition for its own endless sake, but the approximation of appearance to a static and perfect reality. He must, too, take that goal as his own. If he does, he can aid the world and himself by giving rational direction to an otherwise defective teleology. He can, for example, use the reproductive instincts of cattle—or human beings—to breed a superior stock that would never come about on its own initiative. If he ever exercises his powers in any express way, it will be because he knows that his aim as a breeder is really the same as the telos of the animals he breeds—a telos that does not lie, as they dumbly suppose, in merely duplicating themselves, but rather in evolving generation after generation into clearer likenesses of the Forms that they can always more clearly resemble, although never fully match. The human guidance of the divine is for Plato merely a knowledgeable and sympathetic cooperation of intelligence with instincts that fail to see their basic purpose, tied as they are to the pursuit of the past, familiar gratifications that accompany change. For that knowledge and sympathy to exist, however, certain conditions have to be met. The human animal breeder must, obviously, have knowledge of the Forms. He must, too, want the world to resemble them as best it can. He must be like the Form beholding *demiourgos* of the *Timaeus*, who improves on the world's disorderly art because of his preference for the superior features of reality. To be like that figure in terms of knowledge, the animal breeder has to be something ontologically supernatural, for there is no way, according to the *Phaedo*, that a mere organism can behold the Forms. They are never seen in his life, only recollected from a previous existence. Thus there is in Plato a linkage of everything human with something ontologically supernatural. To be like the *demiourgos* in terms of his sympathies, the animal breeder must also be free of control by the organic instincts, which tend to recognize only the endless duration of the earth as their good. He must be supernatural in a teleological as well as ontological sense. He must love the features of reality more than he loves the features of appearance. Otherwise he would not consider the world to be in need of his aid. He must, then, respond to an otherwordly, thanatological impulse. Without feeling that impulse he would not be moved to aid the botched, unintelligent work of the erotic instincts. Thus, an essential ingredient in a fully rational, human teleology is a commitment to *thanatos*—that principle which always seeks a terminal goal beyond the processes of life.

In the ways just outlined Plato comes to associate what he calls human design, or culture, with intelligence, industry, a supernatural agency, and the force of *thanatos*. In contrast, he associates what he calls divine design, or nature, with irrationality, sexual reproduction, a purely natural agency, and the force of *eros*. These clusters of distinctions appear to arise from the inability of appearances to attain the ultimate goal of the motion that soul is always originating. In their frustration they fall into disorder—changing more than they need to change and participating less than they could in class-determining traits. They also come to prefer the pleasures of process, desiring change more than the changeless features of reality. Thus they stand in need of aid from a source beyond themselves. Human art supplies that aid. The divine and the human, then, are related teleologically as the more defective is related to the less defective. Man brings to rational fulfillment—so far as is possible—the paradoxical, impossible aims of earthly change.

Man's Relation to Nature

Plato's teleological doctrines have an important bearing on what it means to be a man or a woman. Since we are offspring of divine workmanship, and subject to the same disorderly vagaries endemic to the rest of the terrestrial plant and animal kingdom, we must in some sense be divine. Yet we are also something human. We thus appear to be a duality of things, subject to contrasting needs, instincts, and fates. That is, indeed, precisely how Plato describes us. Our personalities are really societies of agencies with differing abilities and ambitions. The rational and the less than rational parts of the teleology of appearance meet in us. As a result, we are subject to psychic conflict, and we are not the unities we may think we are.

The question of where we divide into human and divine parts is a question to which a clear, theoretical answer can easily be given. We are human only to the extent that we are supernatural in both ontological status and teleological ambition. The supernatural is not a mere mark of our humanity but its essential, definitive feature. The explanation for why the supernatural is the human is linguistic. Ordinary speech habits find no fault with identifying some faculties and actions as both human and natural. For example, it is both a natural and a human activity to reproduce—or so we think. Once, however, all natural processes are defined as divine, nothing can be called human that was once called natural. *Human* and *divine* are contrasting adjectives, whereas *human* and *natural* are not. In the context of Plato's cosmology, all that is ordinarily considered natural about a man ceases to be human. His humanity is simply what is left after everything natural is taken away.

The question of just what activities and faculties are not natural, and so human, is more difficult to answer. Ordinary speech habits are of little use. Still, Plato's position is fairly clear. His basic principle appears to be that everything about us with an analogue in the plant and animal kingdoms is natural, and so divine. The abilities to reproduce, grow, move, and perceive are abilities we share with at least some other organisms; they are not, therefore, human abilities. Only what is unique about us can be human. Plato does not offer anything like an official, exhaustive list of what he thinks is unique about us. It is clear, however, what he would place at the head of any such list: our abilities to speak, to think, and to act against the grain of instinctual impulse for the sake of some disinterested, moral purpose. As a practical matter for Plato the humanity of a person is exhausted by his intellectual and moral faculties. It is man's conscience and his mind—what Plato calls his reason—that make him human. On the principle that what is human is supernatural, these two faculties make up what the *Phaedo* calls the soul, or *psyche*, of a human being, for the soul is precisely that which is eternal, rational, and counternatural in us. We are, then, divided into human and divine parts, where our souls are divided from everything else about us.

In order to be clear about Plato's psychology, it should be noted that he uses the word *divine* to describe a large number of things, including the Forms and the human soul as well as the *demiourgos* and the cosmos itself. Why so many things are divine is clear: all indestructible things deserve to be called divine. Being divine in this sense, however, does not make the soul, or reason, responsive to a divine teleology. On the contrary, it is precisely because the soul is essentially indestructible that it can escape that drive to participate in immortality through reproduction which Plato associates with the divine art of nature. Being immortal, it has no need to participate in immortality. It has an attribute that participation can never give it. The contrast between the human and the divine should therefore always be understood in teleological terms. What is human about us is immortal and therefore divine, but it does not produce as a primary cause anything belonging to the order of nature. Neither does it respond to a biological teleology. It is in this sense that the human soul is not divine.

It has seemed to many of Plato's commentators that his division of man into two basic parts is a division between the soul and the body. Grube, for example, argues that Plato's psychological duality in the *Phaedo* is a duality between body and soul.[8] Guthrie would seem to agree.[9] Since Plato classes everything biological as divine, there is obvious point to this view. It is, however, a misleading, imprecise view. The distinction between the human and the divine is ultimately a distinction in agency and telos. Whatever is of human design must be traced to a human agency: the reason or soul; whatever is of divine design must be traced to a divine agency. The body of a man, being a product of divine workmanship, is thus designed by and responsive to an agency different from his soul. Consequently, the soul is to be contrasted, not merely to the body, but to the body's designer. The relation of the human soul to the divine is the relation of one artisan to another artisan. It is that point which is obscured by treating Plato's division of man as a division between soul and body.

According to the *Phaedo* (62 B), the *Phaedrus* (250 C) and the *Cratylus* (400 B-C). the soul, or reason, is housed in an

8. G. M. A. Grube, *Plato's Thought* (Boston: Beacon Press, 1958), chap. 4.
9. W. K. C. Guthrie, *A History of Greek Philosophy* (Cambridge: University Press, 1962), 3: 472-81.

alien body in the way a prisoner is kept in protective custody in a jail. The divine artifact to which the human soul is remanded for safekeeping, however, is not an inanimate storage bin. It is part of an organic, living cosmos with needs, ambitions, and instincts of its own. The jail-like body is filled with desires peculiar to itself (*Phaedo* 82 C). In the *Gorgias* (493 A-E) the bodily desires are compared to a leaky jar because of their insatiable quality. Placed in such a container, the soul is obliged to contend with more than a material prison. It has to adapt to another agency, and that is its greatest problem. It is hunger, thirst, anger, pleasure, greed, and lust—not a mere fleshy membrane—that the soul is apt to find disagreeable and alien. Plato never pictures the division within a man as a division between body and soul only. He always pictures it as a teleological conflict between agencies with differing needs and sometimes rival ambitions. In the *Phaedrus* (246 A), for example, he compares the body to a chariot in which the soul, or reason, rides. Horses pulling the chariot do not always respond to the soul's wishes and so the conflict is between rider and living animal, not rider and inanimate vehicle. In the *Philebus* (35C-D) Plato makes the same point explicit. Desire and pleasure are always experienced by a soul, never by the body itself.

If, because of its standing as a mere artifact, the body cannot be the same as what Plato calls the divine element in our make up, what can? The basic answer to this question would seem already to be clear: the erotic instincts—the very instincts whose works are incomplete and in need of aid. They are responsible for organic reproduction, and so for all the artifacts that populate the living realm of nature's divine art. They encompass what the *Symposium* (206 C) and the *Laws* (721 C) call the divine and immortal in us, and they are the forces that Plato most strongly contrasts to the reasonable, honorable, and thanatological impulses of the soul in the *Timaeus* (91 B-C), *Phaedrus* (254 A-B), and *Republic* (571 D; 587 B). Since, too, the metaphysics of the *Timaeus* is designed to equate sexuality with divine portraiture, the conclusion seems inescapable that the erotic instincts are, indeed, the prime carriers of the world's divine teleology. Plato also associates other life-preserving instincts, such as the desire to eat and drink, with forces opposed to the soul (*Phaedo* 81 B), but the erotic, incestuous appetites are the ones most often depicted as offensive to both mind and conscience. Thus they are the chief example of the conservative teleological force opposed to everything human about us.

If the human and the divine components in a man are related as the impulses of his soul are related to his life-sustaining instincts, then one would expect everyone to be in conflict with himself. Everyone is. The soul, at least when it is purified, longs for release from the body it is jailed in (*Phaedo* 67 D-E). All men are subject to contrasting thanatological and erotic forces. These are the forces that represent, first, the true teleology of appearance, which seeks to give becoming the superior features of being; and second, the unintelligent, pleasure-seeking version of that teleology which tends to ignore being and simply seeks to maintain becoming as it is, and for its own sake, forever. Although like the *demiourgos* of the *Timaeus* in terms of its loyalities and tasks, the human soul is unlike the *demiourgos* in being jailed within the teleologically defective realm its role is to improve. Its world is a cave-prison of defective art, and so is the body that immediately surrounds it. For it to bring order out of disorder is for this reason very difficult. It tends to forget its true telos in favor of the instinctual pleasures internal to its companion body (*Phaedo* 83 A-D). It often becomes the first accessory to its own imprisonment.

But even when it does not forget its true telos, its task remains hard. The rival impulses directing the body are difficult to educate to their own, ultimate goals, which lie beyond organic pleasures. The result of trying to rule them may be discord in the personality. Indeed, there is a sense in which every man is always in a state of internal warfare with himself (*Laws* 626 E). The reason and the appetites contend in us all for control of our chariotlike bodies.

The doctrine that a person must be considered a society of agencies because the two aspects of the world's teleology meet in him is of central importance, not just to Plato's psychological theory, but to his moral, aesthetic, and political theory as well. The true teleology of appearance cannot be preserved unless the agency governing the work of man is the reason, or supernatural soul. Knowledge of, and primary allegience to reality is essential if the true telos of change is to be kept intact. The only part of man with the necessary qualifications to guide change is the thanatological reason. That is the implicit point to virtually all the lessons Plato offers his reader in the fields of ethics, art, and politics. Plato is thus wedded to the thesis that each of us is a society of agencies with differing loyalties that readily produce mental conflict. Indeed, his thesis is that we are actually a society of three agencies. In addition to the reason and the appetites, a "spirited" part of the personality must be recognized (*Republic* 435-42; *Phaedrus* 246 B; *Timaeus* 87 A).

Plato always describes the third agency of the mind as having no purpose of its own. He pictures it as something animal and inhuman—a dog in the *Republic* (440 D) and a horse in the *Phaedrus* (246 B)—and therefore something natural or divine. Still, it always responds to the leadership of either the reason or the appetites in the way a trained dog will sometimes obey its master and sometimes its own bestial drives. Consequently, it does not add to the teleological conflict our personalities are subject to. It remains a monstrous "winged drone" (*Republic* 573 A). Thus, although its presence renders us tripartite, we remain divided into but a duality of loyalties. The distinction between the spirit and the other agencies of the personality clearly has an ontological, not teleological, source. In addition to having no purpose of its own, it lacks all knowledge, having opinions only, and is therefore never in the position of an agency that could behold the Forms. The Form-beholding reason is teleologically superior to the appetites but ontologically superior to the spirit. It is related to the appetites as intelligence and conscience are related to irrationality and impulse; but it is related to the spirit as thought and knowledge are related to sensation and opinion. Clearly, the ontological and teleological distinctions Plato uses to combat scientific and moral skepticism determine his psychology. In trying to see just how that determination is made, however, it is necessary to understand that Plato is, indeed, committed to a tripartite theory of the personality.

The Immortality of the Soul and an Obscurity in Plato's Psychology

Plato emphasizes the social character of man's mind so strongly that it cannot be denied without charging him with inconsistency. Still, it is a doctrine that many of his interpreters have found to be incompatible with an important argument given in the *Phaedo* (78 C) for the immortality of the soul. There the soul's immortality is said to be a function of its essentially indivisible, unitary, and therefore indestructible nature. Destruction is only a kind of breaking of things apart, but the soul has no parts and cannot be destroyed. The unity of the soul would seem to conflict with the doctrine that each man is a society of three agencies.

One might conclude from the apparent discrepancy in Plato's work—as many have done—that Plato has no consistent psychological theory. Grube, for example, has argued that Plato's descriptions of the soul vary dramatically from dialogue to dialogue. First, in the *Phaedo*, it is unitary and distinct from the body; then, in the *Symposium*, it becomes nothing separate from the body at all; still later, in the *Republic*, it is tripartite and only partially separate from the body. Grube's conclusion is that a troubled Plato could not arrive at a settled psychological doctrine.[10]

But caution is in order here. Plato is not so changeable in his descriptions of the soul as he at first glance seems to be. Even in the *Republic*, where the social character of the mind is the basis of political lessons Plato is anxious to draw, the supernatural soul of a man is still said to be unitary. Enmeshed, like the sea god Glaucus, in organic accretions, it may appear to be a divisible, broken, mutilated thing from out of the ocean to which the parts of other forms of life have attached themselves—and so appear to be teeming with diversity and contradiction within itself. But beneath its accretions of seaweed and shells it remains in its truest nature something whole and unitary (*Republic* 611 B-D). There is, then, no official discrepancy between the *Phaedo* and the *Republic*. In each dialogue what is supernatural about a man is his unitary, indivisible soul. It may appear to be multiple and divisible, but that is only because our vision of it is marred by the organic accretions of plant and animal life that surround it. Clearly Plato himself is not prepared to accept the judgment that he vacillates in his theory of the

10. Grube, *Plato's Thought*, pp. 147-49.

mind. He acknowledges the apparent discrepancy, but only to stress the unity of doctrine beneath it.

As a way of doing justice to Plato's convictions, one must bear in mind the stringent bonds that tie his psychology to his ontology and his teleology. The world of appearance is a realm of art. Everything visible in it is an artifact. But artifacts presuppose the existence of an agency to design them. Plato identifies that agency with the principle of soul—a principle he declares to be the primal source of all change (*Laws* 892 A). Thus soul has a basic cosmological function in Plato's metaphysics. It moves and designs appearance. Appearance, however, is obviously of different kinds. Some particulars we call products of nature; some we call products of culture. Some must represent the Forms directly; others can only represent appearances like themselves. In acknowledgment of these facts Plato distinguishes between kinds of soul. Since every man and woman can participate in the creation of all kinds of appearance, Plato feels obliged to recognize in each of us a multiple agency.

When the *Sophist* (265 E-266 E) identifies the world of appearance as art, the point is made that every created thing is to be classified in the way we classify a painting: in terms of its model and also it maker. Thus, just as we speak of a Cézanne still life or a Gauguin landscape, so Plato writes of all particulars as having a certain designer and a certain subject matter. Those two features of a particular amount to the ontological and teleological circumstances of production that are of central importance to his cosmology. A particular may be either an *original* or an *imitation* and may have either a *divine* or a *human* agent as its maker. By an original Plato means something that represents a Form directly; by an imitation he means something obviously pictorial that represents another particular. By way of examples, houses are human originals; pictures of a house are human imitations; animal bodies and trees are divine originals; reflections of living things in water are divine imitations. These examples illustrate the four basic categories that all the particulars of appearance fall into. Thus model and agency fix the position of every empirical entity as follows:

HUMAN	DIVINE	
House	Animal	ORIGINALS
Picture of a house	Reflection of an animal	IMITATIONS

Plato's psychological theory maps onto this cosmological schema. The bodily appetites responsible for reproduction are associated with a divine, conservative agency. The reason, being what is supernatural about us in telos as well as in status, is associated with a human agency that adds industrial and architectural artifacts to the world. Both agencies create what Plato calls originals. Since the third agency of the mind, the idle spirit, always cooperates with either the the reason or the appetites, it has a derivative status. It lacks the knowledge necessary to act on its own initiative, and it has to be associated with ignorant imitators whom Plato patronizes as persons requiring the advice of others. The doctor or legislator who has to look up in a manual what to do for a patient or populace is, for Plato, an unknowing imitator who represents appearances and who is bound to produce only a semblance of health or of justice. Likewise, all painters and poets lack knowledge in Plato's judgment; accordingly, they are also imitators. When applied to the schema of the *Sophist*, his point about the spirit's lack of knowledge makes it responsible for all imitations. Thus the correspondence between the equation of appearance with art and Platonic psychological theory can be diagramed with agencies placed in the areas of their productive responsibilities as follows:

HUMAN	DIVINE	
(Reason)	(Appetites)	ORIGINALS
(Spirit)		IMITATIONS

Every normal person can reproduce himself; he can make industrial implements that have no counterparts in the organic realm we call nature; he can also draw pictures of himself and his tools. He can, therefore, manufacture artifacts that fall into all the categories of creation Plato's cosmology recognizes. Since those categories are associated with—even defined by—three kinds of agency, Plato draws the obvious conclusion that every normal person is actually a society of three agents—a society that reflects within its structure the two crucial ontological and teleological distinctions between reality and appearance and the human and the divine. Plato's conclusion is not the result of vacillation or speculation; neither is it abandoned in the face of doubts. He draws it as a straightforward consequence of his basic metaphysical position that everything is pictorial art.

But if the mind really is of three parts, one may ask, why do the *Phaedo* and parts of the *Republic* describe the soul as unitary? The answer is that Plato thinks the soul is unitary. What those dialogues call the unitary soul is the reason—the purely human, supernatural component of the mind that responds to the force of *thanatos*. It is a unity, but its property is not the property of the entire personality. Crucial to this answer, of course, is the assumption that soul for Plato can refer to the reason as well as to the tripartite personality taken as a whole. Plato certainly uses it in both senses. In the *Republic* the soul is first described as a compound of three parts, then carefully declared to be a unity hidden beneath organic accretions that make it appear to be a thing of diversity. A fair reading of Plato's text is that a duality of reference, not a duality of doctrine, is involved. *Soul*, or *psyche*, can mean both "reason" and "personality."

If this reading is accurate, and if the immortal and unitary soul of the *Phaedo* is the reason, then one should be able to find evidence that even the *Phaedo*—with its insistence on the unity of the "psyche"—recognizes other parts of the triadic personality. Evidence of that kind is easily found. Philosophy, Socrates declares, offers to the soul liberation from all the desires that fasten it to the world of becoming (*Phaedo* 82 C). Those desires stem from such biological needs as to eat, drink, and reproduce (*Phaedo* 64 D; 81 B). The soul, being indestructible and immortal, obviously has no such needs of its own. Consequently, the desires of the soul differ from the desires that sustain life. The reason, in short, differs in its teleology from the appetites. The two main components of the tripartite personality are clearly recognized.

The third component is also recognized. Near the beginning of the *Phaedo* (60 C-61 D) Socrates' friends, visiting him before his execution, ask why he has been putting the fables of Aesop to verse. Socrates answers that throughout his life he has obeyed an order coming to him in dreams to practice and cultivate the arts. Previously he had obeyed his dreams by practicing philosophy, the greatest of the arts, but now he feels that a popular form of art might be what his dreams meant. So, to clear his conscience, he has taken up the writing of poetry. The distinction Socrates draws here between the arts is a distinction between those cultivated by the reason and those cultivated by the spirit. Philosophy is the greatest of the arts because it is practiced by the supernatural soul of a man and because its subjects are the Forms. Popular art, however, is invariably a form of "empirical portraiture" that merely imitates the original art of appearance. Thus the agency in control of it is the idle, ontologically derivative spirit which, in having no knowledge and no telos of its own, always imitates the work of others. The point of Socrates' penitential efforts to write poetry during the last days of his life would seem to be that throughout his life he had neglected one of the agencies of his tripartite personality. One of the themes of the *Phaedo* is that a man has obligations to all parts of himself. His chief loyality should be to his reason, of course, for that agency serves to keep intact the world's teleology. It is the rightful ruler of everything else. Still, it is wrong to neglect the needs and appetites of the organic body. Suicide, for example, violates an obligation to the divinities who have placed us on earth (*Phaedo* 62 B). It is wrong, too, to neglect the impulse of the spirit to imitate. Before Socrates drinks his hemlock, he tries to cleanse himself of any slight he has done those agencies of his personality which in his pure, human form he is about to leave. Writing poetry is his way of honoring his spirit.

The psychological theory of the *Phaedo* is the same as that of the *Republic*, the *Phaedrus*, and the other dialogues that describe the personality as tripartite. The reason, the appetites, and the spirit are all present. Plato's theory reflects throughout his career the basic distinctions of his cosmology. The word *soul* does have a dual reference for him, as he himself would seem to point out in the *Republic*. There is, however, no duality of doctrine. Plato always recognizes the personality as tripartite; he always recognizes the human reason as unitary.

I now want to strengthen the force of these conclusions by showing how Plato's aesthetic theory aligns itself with his vision of man as a society of three.

4

Aesthetics–The Divine Alliance of Spirit and Opinion

The Classification of the Arts

The *Sophist*'s division of all particulars into originals and imitations of either human or divine design gives Plato the principles he uses to classify the arts. Some arts—such as those of industry and architecture—add to what already exists in the world. Some arts—such as those of poetry and painting—merely imitate what already exists. Plato calls the art of adding *autopoiesis*, or original-making; the art of imitating is *eidolopoiesis*, or image-making (*Sophist* 266 A). Since an original represents a Form and an image represents another particular, the distinction between arts rest on a difference in productive circumstances. Whether a given artifact is the result of adding or of imitating depends solely upon its subject matter. If one can show that it represents reality, then it must be an original. If one can show that it represents some aspect of appearance, then it must be an imitation. There is, of course, no third possibility. The difference between reality and appearance is the cardinal difference in Plato's metaphysics. It is a difference that cannot be annulled. Thus an artifact's model is either a Form or another particular. It cannot be both.

Although the duality of possible models for an artifact cannot be annulled, the duality of possible agencies the *Sophist* recognizes can. There is the possibility—illustrated by the work of the animal breeder—of a human and a divine agent's cooperating to make a single particular. Plato calls a cooperative venture of this kind the aiding of appearance. It is a form of production in which human and divine agents share credit for the artifact they make. It can issue only in an original or an image, and so it is always a specialized form of adding to what exists or of imitating what has already been made. It is, however, sufficiently distinctive to have a name of its own, and so Plato adopts a triadic classification of the arts: adding to appearance, aiding it, and imitating it (*Sophist* 219 A-B; *Laws* 889 D).

The human art of adding to, without aiding, what exists is the basic art of culture. Its chief feature is that what is created has no counterpart in the order of nature. The notion of adding thus has both an ontological and teleological significance. The ontological significance is that a Form is represented. The teleological significance is that the Form represented is one that nothing in nature also represents. Since nature is a realm bent on reproducing itself, the clear import of Plato's stand is that only what exists apart from the divine teleology of the world can invent. Novelty is the prerogative of the supernatural. Consequently, Plato associates it with the ethically sensitive reason of man. Examples of additive, exclusively human, and novel forms of production come from the industrial arts, including the making of spindles, beds, shoes, and harnesses (*Cratylus* 389 B; *Republic* 597 D; 601 C). These articles are all inventions of man. They are not found in the incomplete realm of nature, and they do not respond to its teleology. They also require in Plato's view a meta-empirical knowledge for their manufacture. Since that knowledge is a monopoly of the reason, and the reason is the distinctively human element of man's personality, a supernatural agency always adds to nature. Plato's favorite example of the additive artisan is not, however, the industrial worker, but the Promethean architect, or master builder, who directs a crew of workers and erects the buildings in which man lives apart from nature. Knowing the use of the ship's hull that separates man from the sea or the purpose of the house that shelters him from the elements, together with having control of a crew of workmen, the architect combines to some degree the expert knowledge and political power of those who should rule the state. He is thus a fitting example of what a wise king should be like (*States*man 260 A-C.)—a point, by the way, on which Athenians would seem to be in need of instruction, for although they require their architects and teachers to be men of expert knowledge, they make no similar demands on those who offer political advice (*Protagoras* 319 B-D).

The art of aiding nature will make use of Forms already manifest in the world. It therefore does not involve invention, but it still may have an important cultural function. Because nature is as deficient as it is incomplete, it stands in need of help—help that the aiding arts of culture can supply. The basic examples of those arts are medicine, animal husbandry, agriculture, and gymnastics (*Laws* 889 D; *Sophist* 219 A; *Republic* 459 A; *Philebus* 56 B). Each is of two kinds. When, for instance, the physician knows what he is doing, and so remembers the Form the body he is seeking to cure represents, he is a true scientist with a genuine skill. He has what deserves to be called art. When, however, he does not know what he is doing and looks, not directly to a Form, but to a deficient particular for his model, he is nothing but a quack who frequently harms his patients and who, at best, makes only a semblance (*eidolon*) of health (*Laws* 720 A-B; *Gorgias* 463 D). He has only what deserves to be called an unteachable, empirical knack (*Gorgias* 463 B). He is akin to the painter and poet who lack knowledge and merely imitate what already exists. The wise ruler of an ideal state—who would act as both physician to its citizens and their breeder—should not, therefore, be proficient in this bogus version of aiding nature. He must, on the contrary, know how truly to improve on what exists by being able to add to it. Thus, just as the intellect supplements and clarifies the testimony of the senses, so the head of a well-run state will make good the omissions and correct the errors of the organic world. Plato's epistemological and cultural theories are mirror images of each other.

Plato's ideas about the arts that add to and aid nature require little comment. Some commentators, to be sure, have ignored Plato's discussion of the additive arts. Lovejoy's claim that all Forms necessarily manifest themselves in appearance fails to recognize even the existence of an additive art for Plato.[1] Lodge, too, claims that Plato says not one word about a nonmimetic art.[2] But these claims are simply false. Some art, Plato insists, adds to appearance; only some imitates. Yet, apart from the need to stress that Plato does, indeed, recognize the existence of an additive group of arts, there is little that has to be said about his views. His discussions of industrial and architectural designs as additions to the world are clear, and few of those who have dealt with this subject have found it puzzling. His doctrines on the arts that aid nature are also clear. The claim of the *Sophist* and the *Republic* that one kind of art, or knack, imitates what exists, including natural objects, has,

1. Lovejoy, *The Great Chain of Being*, p. 52.
2. R. C. Lodge, *Plato's Theory of Art* (London: Routledge and Kegan Paul, 1953), p. 74.

however, created virtually universal perplexity among Plato's interpreters. Their reaction to his claim calls for an extended analysis of his use of the term *mimesis*, or "imitation."

The Doctrine of Imitation

Very few modern critics or philosophers would care to defend the doctrine that the fine arts are literally imitative of nature. Its falsity seems so patent that it is usual, indeed, to attribute it to no one and to claim instead that the notion of artistic imitation must have been understood by Plato in some nonliteral sense. Bosanquet, for example, claimed years ago that for Plato an imitation was not a full reproduction of an original, as one might most naturally expect, but a mere semblance of a real thing.[3] Collingwood insisted that the meaning of *mimesis* is precisely not its literal one of "imitation."[4] McKeon, too, has held that at no time is *mimesis* established in a literal sense in any of the Platonic dialogues.[5] Beardsley,[6] Murphy[7] and Havelock[8] all echo the same judgment.

In spite of the many efforts to divest Plato of what seems to be too improbable a thesis for anyone to have held, his

3. Bernard Bosanquet, *A History of Aesthetic* (New York: Meridian Books, 1957), p. 28.
4. R. G. Collingwood, "Plato's Philosophy of Art," *Mind* 34 (1925): 154-72.
5. Richard McKeon, "Literary Criticism and the Concept of Imitation in Antiquity," *Modern Philology* 34 (1936): 1-35.
6. M. C. Beardsley, *Aesthetics from Classical Greece to the Present* (New York: Macmillan, 1966), p. 34.
7. N. R. Murphy, *The Interpretation of Plato's Republic* (Oxford: The Clarendon Press, 1951), p. 224.
8. E. A. Havelock, *Preface to Plato* (Cambridge, Mass.: Harvard University Press, 1963), pp. 20-34. Havelock finds the use of the word *mimesis* so peculiar and misleading that he accuses Plato of having no understanding of what art and poetry are and, consequently, of having no aesthetic theory! In that judgment he has, as he notes, the support of many modern scholars, including Shorey, Cassirer, Ritter, and Friedlander.

account of the fine arts is a well-formulated consequence of his cosmology. His term *mimesis* is best understood without interpretive emendations in the normal sense of the English word *imitation*. Virtually all translators of Plato admit that *mimesis* does translate most readily as "imitation." They merely argue that for Plato it had some puzzling, special sense. The only major critic to challenge the usual translation is Koller, who argues that *mimesis* was originally used to refer to the expressive quality of music and that Plato perversely extended its use to poetry, giving it an invidious sense.[9]

In a rebuttal of Koller's thesis, Else has listed the fifth-century uses of *mimesis* in what surviving texts there are. He points out that the *mimos*, or cult actor, had something to do with the sound effects produced by those who wielded various instruments, such as the bull roarer. *Mimesis* was connected with music, therefore, not because music was particularly expressive of feeling, but because its sounds duplicated natural ones, especially the sounds of animals. Thus Pindar refers to the imitation in song of a siren's voice and gorgon's cry. Other writers use the term to refer to one person's imitating the actions of another by duplicating his feat, as Cleisthenes imitated his grandfather, according to Herodotus, when he invaded Attica. *Mimesis* would seem to translate as "imitation."

After replying to Koller, Else goes on to argue in the usual fashion that Plato's language is peculiar and that he "forges a new concept of 'imitation.'"[10] Plato's use of *mimesis* certainly seems to differ from that of writers before his time, but one is not entitled to think that a new concept is involved for that reason. An unusual theory about empirical things determines Plato's usage, and one cannot under-

9. Herman Koller, *Die Mimesis in der Antike* (Bern: Francke, 1954).
10. G. F. Else, "Imitation in the Fifth Century," *Classical Philology* 53 (1958): 73-90.

stand the meanings of his language apart from a consideration of his philosophical theses. In the context of an unusual cosmology words are bound to have unusual usages, but that does not itself make their meanings different. Plato's use of the word *mimesis* fits very well the apparent meaning of the same word before his time. In the use Plato makes of it when discussing the arts, it certainly corresponds to the meaning of the English word *imitation*.

To explain why Plato's aesthetic doctrines should be taken at face value, a comment on English usage is in order, for it is the supposed discrepancy between the Platonic *mimesis* and the English *imitation* that produces the nigh universal warnings of modern translators not to take their renderings literally. Even the most cursory review of the word *imitation* reveals two obvious reasons for their objections to the claim that a work of fine art can be imitative of nature. First, that claim does not meet the requirement that an imitation artifact be of the same class of objects as the original on which it is modeled. There is no similar requirement for imitation materials, for an imitation diamond is glass or paste; a piece of imitation leather is plastic or fiber; and imitation ice cream is made of substitutes for real cream. If, however, one were to imitate a Cassini gown, an actual gown would have to be sewn. Likewise, a magazine publisher, jeweler, or appliance manufacturer may imitate the products of his competitors, but in doing so his imitations would be actual magazines, or genuine pieces of jewelry, or real appliances. In no case would the artifact that is an imitation of another be a mere image, semblance, or representation of it. A picture of a natural scene is not, then, an imitation of its subject, for the trivial reason that it is a picture, while its subject is not. Only when an artist uses some other artist's painting as a stylistic model for his own is one of the essential conditions met for rightly calling his work an imitation.

A second objection to the claim that art imitates nature is implicit in the examples given. It is by no means obvious that someone is responsible for the design of nature, yet when anyone makes an artifact that is an imitation of something else, some other agent is imitated. Indeed, when an artifact is identified as an imitation, it is done so by mentioning the name of the agent responsible for the design of the original. It makes sense, for example, to speak of an imitation Cassini gown, though not just of an imitation gown. Whom the artist has imitated thus needs to be cited when calling his work imitative. It is, however, at best a speculative theory that an artist's natural subjects are products of an agent; and so for this reason, too, Plato's doctrine has seemed to be obviously false if interpreted literally.

Yet the very grounds that have made translators wary of Plato's language are precisely the grounds for thinking that "imitation" is an acceptable translation of his word *mimesis*. That nature is divine, representational art is his basic cosmological thesis; in the context of that thesis it clearly makes sense to identify the landscape painter as an imitator. He creates an artifact that is the same kind of thing, a picture, as that produced by the divine agent he imitates. Since the circumstances of production alone determine what class a particular belongs to, it is clear that they are all ontologically the same kind of thing: pictorial appearances. The aesthetic doctrines of the *Republic* and the *Sophist* need to be taken quite literally. The making of an image in water or on a draftsman board is imitation only because the originals are, like everything in the cosmos, themselves images.

The claim that art is imitative would apply, of course, only to artifacts that are by common consent representational of empirical models. A direct picturing of the Forms would not be imitation in any literal sense. Forms are not the work of some artist, and they cannot be duplicated. Only a pictorial copying of the pictorial art work of appearance can be imitation. Thus Plato is anxious to explain what he means by *imitation* by using the example of empirical portraiture (*Republic* 596 E). Because he wishes to call poetry, music, dance, and the other fine arts imitative as well, he tries to fix painting as the prototype of them all. Most of his discussions of the imitative "arts" that are really "knacks" link them to painting. The discussion of the mimetic character of music in the *Laws* (668 B-C) ends in the claim that composers and listeners alike would all agree that its productions are a form of empirical portraiture. That dance is representational of sensory models is affirmed as well (*Laws* 798 D-E). Likewise, the discussion of the difference between narrative and imitative poetry in the early part of the *Republic* (393 C-D) centers on the point that the imitative poet represents by assimilating his voice and bearing to that of another, while the simple narrator does not. In the tenth book of the *Republic* the representational, rhythmic adornments of poetry are held responsible for all its charms, so that it becomes essentially an imitative art, and so akin to painting (601 A-C). Poetry produces, not originals, but only images *(eidola)* that do not require knowledge for their production. Given the point that the fine arts represent the original art of the empirical world, the claim stands that they are literally imitative of their subjects. The inherent implausibility of Plato's position vanishes if one comes to see the world as he describes it.

Yet, there is another reason why scholars have been reluctant to accept a literal rendition of *mimesis*. Since Plato says that an empirical portrait is thrice removed from the truth (*Republic* 597 E; 602 C), many commentators on the *Republic* have concluded that in his view the artist imitates originals that are themselves mere imitations of reality. Their conclusion does require one, at least sometimes, not to take *mimesis* literally, for a particular is drastically unlike a Form for Plato and could not actually be a copy as a true imitation would be. There is, however, less evidence for the view that particulars imitate Forms than is often supposed, and—in any event—the artist's effort to represent appearance with other appearances would remain literally imitative. The *Sophist* is clear about this matter. There the making of originals that represent Forms is called adding, and *mimesis* remains the distinct process of representing the particulars of appearance (235 B-C). In spite of the clarity of Plato's text, Grube, Carritt, McKeon, Butcher, Friedlander, Crombie, Lodge, Greene, Verdenius, Cornford, Cherniss, and many other modern commentators on Plato accept without argument the view originally put forth by Aristotle (*Metaphysics* 987 b 8-13) that for Plato *imitation* and *participation* are mere synonyms. If so, all particulars are imitations of the Forms, and a literal rendering of *mimesis* must remain in doubt.

The discussion of imitation in the *Republic* fits perfectly well the account given in the *Sophist*. There is little reason to suppose that *methexis*, "participation," means the same as *mimesis*, "imitation." The relations denoted by each term are, of course, representational ones, but the circumstances of production under which the similar relations arise differ. When a particular represents a Form, its relation to its model is that of *methexis*; when one represents another particular, its relation to its model is that of *mimesis*. The account of productive processes in the *Republic* would seem to make this as clear as the account of the *Sophist*. At 597 D in the *Republic* a deity (*theos*) is said to beget or create the Form Couch. In view of the ontological priority of the Form of the Good over other Forms, one may take this deity to be The Good, for no soul, it is said, could ever create a Form (*Republic* 596 B). The representational artist who is a soul needs a preexisting model for his work. Since the Form-creating deity is also a *phytourgos*, or by-nature-maker, the process of creating Forms may be called *phytourgia*. A carpenter using the Form Couch as the model for the empirical couch he makes is a *demiourgos*, or by-culture-maker, and his productive process may be called *demiourgia*, or *demipoiesis*. Since the carpenter's model is an object of knowledge, he produces originals, or *auta*. The painter who uses the carpenter's couch as his model in making a picture is not, however, a *demiourgos*. He is a mere imitator, and since the mimetic poet produces *eidola*, the process involved may be called *eidolourgia*, or *eidolopoiesis*. Three agents, three processes, and three products thus become distinguishable:

Agents:
Phytourgos—The Good
Demiourgos—Industrial Artisan
Eidolourgos—Fine Artisan

Processes:
Phytourgia—Nature or Form Making
Demiourgia—Culture Making (Adding to what exists)
Eidolourgia—Image Making (Imitating what exists)

Products:
Onta—Forms
Auta—Originals
Eidola—Imitations

Considering only those categories which apply to the manufacture of particulars, the classification of the productive arts in the *Sophist* remains intact in the *Republic*. There the only products that are imitations are those which are the same kind of things as their subject matter. Every product not representing the same kind of thing as itself is not an imitation. Since the *phytourgos* has no model for the Form Couch, it cannot imitate. There could be an imitation of a Form only if one could be modeled on another, but the possibility of a plural manufacture of a Form is immediately ruled out by a version of the Third Man argument—a new, third Form with priority over others would arise from a duplication of the Form Couch. So, "by compulsion or by choice," the *phytourgos* makes but one Form for each class of thing. As far as Plato's aesthetics is concerned, there is no possibility of making imitative copies of the Forms. Being cannot be duplicated, and the relation of appearances to reality cannot be that of imitations to an original. Collingwood writes of the human carpenter as imitating or copying the Form Couch,[11] and Grube also suggests that "No doubt the carpenter does, in a sense, 'imitate' the *eidos*."[12] To read Plato in this fashion is to miss or to ignore the distinction between imitating and adding that he himself introduces. It is only the fine artist who imitates.

The key question of how a picture of a tree or of a couch can be an imitation of its subject is still to be answered by pointing out that the so-called real tree, or so-called real couch, is actually a picture itself, produced by a divine or human artisan on the surface of the spatial receptacle. The painter's product is an imitation of another artist's three-dimensional picture, and he copies what has already been done by another without having that knowledge of the Forms that is required for adding something new to the cosmos. Collingwood's interpretation of Plato's use of *mimesis* is clearly incorrect. He writes that misunderstandings of the aesthetic doctrine in the *Republic* arise from assuming that when Socrates speaks of copying he means that kind of activity by which a carpenter makes a chair resembling another chair, or an artist paints a picture resembling another picture. A copy, or an imitation, is, how-

11. Collingwood, "Plato's Philosophy of Art."
12. G. M. A. Grube, *Plato's Thought*, p. 189.

ever," . . . an object of an entirely different order, having the characteristics proper to that order." In the *Republic* Socrates certainly does seem to mean by imitating the copying of something on the same order; if that is not a plausible account of the fine arts, that only indicates the implausibility of the cosmology supporting it.

To bolster his claims, Collingwood argues that the threefold epistemological distinction of the *Republic* corresponds to a threefold ontological distinction between the Forms, appearances of the Forms, and appearances of appearances, which include all imitative artifacts at a third remove from reality with a set of standards and characteristics proper to them. It is clear, however, from the passages at 477 A-B in the *Republic* that knowledge pertains to what is, and ignorance pertains to what is not, while opinion pertains to what lies between. On the basis of that trichotomy, the imitative arts are on the same level as all other particulars, just as the principles of classification used in the *Sophist* dictate. Although they are appearances of appearances, their ontological status is not different from that of all others. A mirror image reflected into another mirror produces just another mirror image. Plato's point is not that imitations are less real than their models; it is, on the contrary, that the empirical models used are just as unreal as their imitations. The whole Platonic account of the comparative unreality of appearance depends upon that point. Plato does not contrast, he compares empirical objects to pictures. Thus one must reject, not just Collingwood's views, but McKeon's conclusion as well, that throughout its varied use *imitation* consistently marks, for Plato, a contrast between the work of imitation and something else, which is, in comparison with it, real.[13] There is no difference in degrees of reality between an artifact and its

13. McKeon, "Literary Criticism and the Concept of Imitation in Antiquity."

poetic imitation. Plato's metaphysics is no more triadic, as Collingwood and McKeon would have it, than it is quadrifid. The allegory of the divided line does not compromise his dualism, and neither does his aesthetics. Just as there is only one kind of thing—Forms—above the line separating appearance from reality, so there is only one kind of thing—pictorial particulars—below it.

The conclusion that the fine arts are no more unreal than their models and that they are literal imitations must stand, even though there is some reason to think that Plato—outside the *Republic* and the *Sophist*—did not always distinguish participation from imitation. In the *Timaeus* he sometimes writes of worldly things as imitations of the Forms. Some of these passages, however, do not of themselves imply that *participation* and *imitation* are synonyms. At 38 A, for example, he says that time revolves according to a law of number and imitates eternity. Since he identifies eternity with the condition of the Forms, one is entitled to think that the temporal world of change is for Plato an imitation of reality. Indeed, he does in later passages identify the cosmos as a whole as a visible imitation of an eternal pattern (48 E). Here, however, Plato is writing of the two realms of appearance and reality as wholes. He is not writing of individual Forms or of the individual particulars that participate in them. This point is of some importance, for taken as a whole the class of all particulars does have important attributes in common with reality—and it would seem to be that fact which Plato is calling attention to in describing the world as an imitation. The entire cosmos is unending in its history; although an organism, it does not die or decay but maintains itself through constant change and reproduction of its parts. Similar to the realities apart from it, the world has the primary marks of deity in being unitary and forever existent. The world of art does succeed to a certain extent in becoming like the Nature it wants to be. Accordingly Plato calls it a god. Just as a society survives the death of each of its members through birth, so the world as a whole abides forever while its mortal parts appear and disappear. It manages, however defectively, to be a visible, moving imitation of the invisible and unchanging Forms its parts merely participate in. It is a moving, multiple image and imitation at once of eternity. Since all movement is a form of creation for Plato, the moving image that is the cosmos is unique; all other, component images arise and disappear, but through change the cosmos as a conglomerate image abides. Thus it acquires characteristics all individual representations of the Forms lack.

The account Plato offers of reproduction indicates that he does distinguish between individual and specific forms of participation. He writes that each member of the race who procreates participates in immortality, but only through his contribution to the continuity of the race that is time's equal twin and companion (*Laws* 721 C). Participation is here a relation between the mortal, apparent members and the immortal whole of an empirical class—a relation analogous to that between a particular and a class-determining Form. Only because the empirical class has attributes that its apparent members lack, and that make it similar in status to a Form, can it as a whole imitate reality and have its members participate in its attributes as they do in the Forms they picture. By contributing to the life of the race one participates in its immortality, but that contribution is participation only because the race has attributes the Form Mankind itself has. The conclusion that Plato uses *imitate* and *participate* synonymously can be drawn from these passages in the *Timaeus* and the *Laws* only with the specious aid of the fallacy of composition.

Still, it may be objected, there are in the *Timaeus* passages that call individuals imitations. At 50 C-D, for example, the offspring of the Forms are *mimetata*. Here is evidence, surely, that Aristotle was right and that *mimesis* and *methexis* are synonyms. Indeed, it is evidence. It is, however, meager evidence that these words are interchangeable in all the dialogues. One can conclude that they are only by ignoring the distinction between adding and imitating that is of central importance to the discussions of art in the *Sophist* and the *Republic*. There, with the utmost clarity, Plato distinguishes between the fine arts and the industrial arts on the ground that the fine artist is a maker of imitations while the industrial artist is not. Since the industrial, additive arts participate directly in the Forms, and the imitative arts do not, there is a distinction between participation and imitation that has to be recognized. In those cases where Plato uses that distinction—all central to his aesthetic theory—the word *mimesis* has the literal sense of "imitation." What the fine artist does is model his work on the no more real but obviously more original art of another. From the point of view of one who sees the whole of life as a set of images, there is no difference in the degree of reality between imitations and originals. Plato's aesthetic doctrine is best understood as the literal claim that the poet imitates his subject. There is no more point in trying to save Plato from his own text here than there is in the case of his puzzling epistemological doctrines.

The Consequences of the Doctrine of Imitation

As already pointed out, the fine arts are imitative for Plato only because they represent particulars. With a change of subject matter they would become modes of original production. Thus Plato does not define them as imitative. Commentators such as Collingwood who claim otherwise are mistaken. Aristotle again seems to be the source of the confusion on this point, for at the beginning of his *Poetics* he does define the representational arts as diverse modes of imitation. Plato, however, does not make that mistake. Whether or not an artifact is an imitation depends upon the circumstances of its production, for—as far as the *Republic* and the *Sophist* are concerned—if it is not copied from a model that is the same kind of artifact as itself, it is not an imitation. It is a perfectly good possibility on Plato's account that a painting be the result of additive, rather than imitative, production—just as it is possible that a carpenter's bed be an imitation of some other carpenter's bed rather than an original image of a Form. Plato has to recognize those possibilities, and he does allow for them in his classification of the productive arts. He seems to hold, however, that as a matter of contingent fact all industrial production is additive and that all the fine arts are imitative.

The reason Plato is loath to admit that there are both imitative and additive architects and painters alike is that he wishes to make his method of classification compatible with ordinary distinctions between representational and nonrepresentational objects. To achieve a compatibility he has to argue that ordinary distinctions between pictorial and nonpictorial artifacts correspond to a constant difference in the circumstances under which those artifacts are made. If a painter or poet ever knew what he was doing—and so had a Form for his model—or if a carpenter ever used an empirical model for a bed, their products would have to be classified in ways that run counter to the ordinary contrast of representational to nonrepresentational art. The painting in Plato's schema would be an original; the bed would be an image. Still, such possibilities are clearly a feature of Plato's method of classifying particulars; and his denial of any ultimate difference between images and actual things on the level of appearance demands an accounting from him.

One carpenter could model his bed on that of another; but in that case his work would be a three-dimensional artifact which, unlike the painter's imitation, could be slept in rather than merely looked at. Thus Plato has to distinguish two kinds of imitation. In the *Sophist* (235 C - 236 C) he does. There he calls a copy, or imitation, that conforms to the proportions in all three dimensions of the original an icon. He calls an unproportioned copy, such as a systematically distorted statue or a two-dimensional painting, a phantasm.[14] Both icons and phantasms are products of *eidolourgia*, or imitation, but Plato uses his distinction to fit cases in which the terms *imitation* and *representation* would normally apply. It is not, however, the same distinction as the one it replaces, and Plato does not construe the difference between imitating and representing as merely a difference between two special kinds of imitating. One would not, normally, call an exact casting of a man's face an imitation of his face; yet one would call a carpenter's bed an imitation that only roughly resembled another's used as a model. Thus Plato's contrast between mere phantasms and icons is not parallel to the ordinary contrast between pictures and actual imitations. He is, indeed, prevented by his cosmology from providing on the level of appearance a contrast that would be. Since his cosmological metaphor has expanded beyond normal usage the conditions for correctly calling something an imitation, the result is that he is forced to call all production using an empirical model imitative. At a point where *imitation* and *representation* usually apply, the only distinction now provided is that between exact and inexact duplication of original works of art. Plato reserves additive, or original, representation for the picturing of

14. Plato does not say what a faithful two-dimensional copy of another copy would be. On the basis of his distinction, as he states it, one painter carefully imitating another's phantasm would create, not another phantasm, but an icon. This embarrassment illustrates the difficulty Plato has in keeping representational and seemingly nonrepresentational artifacts classed apart. In the *Republic* (598 B)

insensible being; it is on that level that the ordinary contrast between picturing and imitating reappears in his system. There is, thus, no confusion between a picture and an actual imitation. Plato does not stretch the sense of *mimesis* to include both. It is a term he does provide with its usual contrast, but on a level different from the normal one.

Plato does not meet all his difficulties with the distinction between icons and phantasms, however, for he cannot use it in practice. A consideration of his classificatory schema, expanded by the inclusion of icons and phantasms, will make his problem clear:

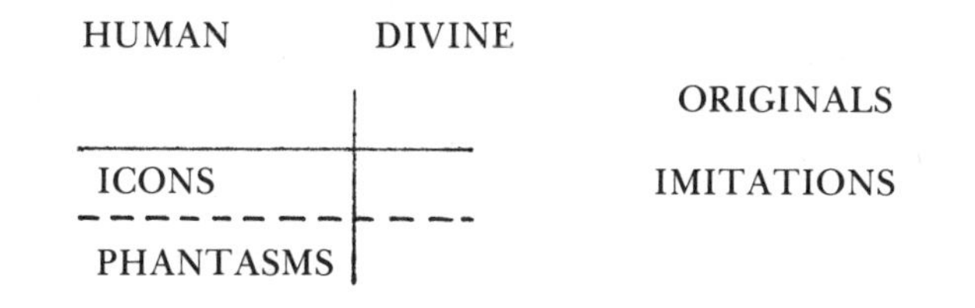

The basic point to keep in mind about Plato's schema is the one already stressed that the categories involved refer only to the circumstances under which a particular is made. They do not refer to the kind, or class, of particular it is. They don't because Plato thinks of all the products of change as ontologically alike. They are, without exception, images. He also thinks that all change is akin to portrait making. Thus he faces the task of introducing analogues of the common-sense distinctions between representational and nonrepresentational objects his cosmological methaphor has obliterated. The tension that results stems from the need to keep what one normally takes to be pictorial objects classed together under the same circumstances

he mentions a two-dimensional imitation of a phantasm that he later (599 A) calls a phantasm as well. What entitles him to call it a phantasm goes unmentioned. Presumably his thesis is that no exact imitations, or icons, exist, and that the question is therefore moot.

of production. Plato's implicit argument is that the metaphysically insignificant distinction of opinion between metaphysically similar products always corresponds to a difference in productive circumstances.

A second point, which is really a consequence of the first, is that the classificatory schema of the *Sophist* has to be expanded further. In the *Sophist* the dialogue centers on an attempt to define the sophist, who is some kind of ignorant imitator. Since he is an imitator, the effort to define him makes no use of subdivisions in the class of originals. But a distinction parallel to that between icons and phantasms must be made. If something produced by a human being represents a Form, it is an original; thus if the model of what is normally taken to be a representational artifact, such as a painting, were a Form, it too would be an original and not an eidolon, or imitation. Because of its obvious representational character, however, it would differ in appearance from other, seemingly nonrepresentational originals. Accordingly, a division within originals parallel to that within imitations has to be recognized. Eight divisions delineate all the theoretical possibilities arising from a conjunction of the common-sense distinction between representational and nonrepresentational art and Plato's metaphysical analysis of productive circumstances. A numbering of the divisions will help to keep a discussion of them clear:

HUMAN	DIVINE	
1. House	2. Animal	ORIGINALS
3. Picture of the Form House	4. Reflection of the Form Animal	
5. House modeled on another house	6. Animal modeled on another animal	IMITATIONS
7. Picture of a house	8. Reflection of an animal	

Of these eight divisions, 4. and 6. are without members of any kind; 3. and 5. are empty of what would normally be expected to be examples, and Plato does not offer clear substitutes. The reasons for his not doing so indicate a great deal about his difficulties in maintaining his cosmological equation of art and nature. Those difficulties explain, in turn, his hostility toward the imitative arts.

There is, first of all, an obvious embarrassment in admitting that icons—sections 5. and 6.—exist. The embarrassment is that they are of the same empirical class as their models. The house made by an apprentice architect who seems to copy a master builder is, after all, a house. Since Plato takes the empirical analogue of class membership to a representational relation between the similar, apparent members of a class and a Form, the apprentice's house must always have for its actual model a Form and not, as seems to be the case, an empirical model. Thus apprentices produce artifacts that participate in Forms and do not imitate other particulars.

Plato's theory of language obliges him to describe all industrial and architectural artifacts as orginals. A common noun is for him the proper name of a Form; therefore all artifacts of any given empirical class are related to a single Form. Since that relation is the pictorial one of participation, all artifacts with the same empirical name must represent the same model in reality. As an explanation for the discrepancy between what seems to be the case and what must be the case when an apprentice designs an industrial implement, Plato relies on the practice of geometry instructors. These teachers will illustrate abstract, conceptual theorems and postulates by drawing figures for their students to study. Plato contends that their figures are meant to be understood only as images or representations of intelligible principles. The sensible figures are not to be treated as models of what the students themselves should draw in their exercises; they are mere heuristic indicators of the intelligible proofs that should be pictured (*Republic* 510 D). Apprentices in any true art must act in a similar way; geometry, for Plato, is the quintessential science, and all who truly learn anything from others must treat their masters' constructions as geometry students treat geometrical drawings—that is, as images, not as models, of what they themselves should represent. Plato thus upgrades the work of all industrial artisans from imitative knack to additive art. The industrial designer, indeed, is Plato's favorite example of one who everybody admits knows what he is doing (*Protagoras* 319 B; *Philebus* 56 B; *Republic* 597 D). Because the industrial designer does have knowledge he must, on Plato's grounds, have Forms for his models. The conclusion follows that the architect and industrial craftsman create originals, not iconic imitations.

The same problem that prevents Plato from admitting that industrial icons, section 5., exist prevents him from admitting that there are natural icons, section 6. Even if one of the muses were to duplicate an animal in all three dimensions, it would not be a mere imitation, but another animal participating in the same Form as its ostensive model. Speaking on this subject in the *Cratylus* (432 B-C) Socrates declares that if some god were to make a copy of a man in all his attributes, the copy would not be an icon, but a second man who deserved the same name as the first. One cannot, therefore, duplicate appearance by imitating it. Anything that seems to be a duplication is actually an original. There are, then, no icons produced either by the gods or by industrial artisans.

For similar reasons no maker of portraits, statues, or other representational artifacts produces an icon. The need to achieve a beautiful effect, Plato explains, requires that he distort his images, so that as a matter of universal practice, not by definition, he produces phantasms instead of icons (*Sophist* 236 A). The prohibition on fine artists' producing icons, or what would normally be accepted as true imitations, extends to both artificial and natural subject matters. Indeed, if a human being were to produce a true, iconic imitation of anything natural, an even greater difficulty would arise in that the distinction between culture and nature would break down. The breakdown would appear in Plato's schema by the failure of certain classes of things to be produced consistently under the same circumstances. Some apparent members of the same class would be of human design, others of divine. Thus there are no Frankensteins or Pygmalions who can imitate nature by duplicating its living creatures through the techniques of art. All representations of nature are distorted phantasms. Plato, it is clear, does not recognize the existence of any icons.

Because Plato's classifications allow for two kinds of imitation, some commentators[15] have claimed that Plato recognizes two kinds of fine art: a good kind, composed of icons, which does not distort its model, and a bad kind, composed of phantasms, which does distort its model. These are indeed theoretical possibilities, but Plato does not recommend the "good" kind of art. The very existence of an undistorted icon would be an embarrassment to him; it would look like an original but actually be an imitation. His concern, therefore, is to establish the point that the industrial arts are made up entirely of originals and that the fine arts are made up entirely of distorted phantasms. No drama, no poem, no painting ever duplicates life.

For a similar reason the fine arts never picture the Forms. The pervasive difficulty Plato faces is that his aesthetic categories are broader than the ones they are generalized

15. For example: K. Gilbert and H. Kuhn, *A History of Esthetics* (New York: Macmillan, 1939), pp. 33-34.

from—as they have to be if all visible things are viewed as products of pictorial art. To prevent a discrepancy between his own classes and the customary ones of common speech and sense, he must deny that where his classes extend beyond those of normal conviction there is anything left in need of classification. Thus he must hold as a factual thesis that industrial apprentices actually add to what exists rather than imitate it, though he admits that they could imitate. The quiet elevation of industrial production to the constant status of additive art has its parallel in a reduction of fine art to the status of imitation, and the reasons are clearly the same. If a portrayal of a Form in a recognized medium of the fine arts actually existed, it would be an original and, in theory, of the same empirical class as functional, three-dimensional objects. The common-sense distinction between representational and nonrepresentational objects would then break down. Therefore both divisions 3. and 5. are empty of anything that is, as a matter of linguistic convention, representational.

Since natural reflections on shiny surfaces always do have some empirical cause and subject matter, Plato need not try to explain away anything that seems to be the case in regard to them. Division 4., where reflections of Forms would go, is empty. For artificial images, however, an important problem exists. It is a perfectly good possibility on Plato's account that the images of fine art should represent Forms. Industrial artisans picture them, and there is no reason why in principle a painter or poet could not do the same. There are several discussions in the dialogues that would seem to admit this possibility while failing to acknowledge that it is ever realized. The most notable case occurs in the *Republic* (472 D), where Plato presents the hypothetical possibility of a painter's drawing an ideally beautiful man. Any such painter, it seems, would have no empirical model for his work. Other, less explicit examples of a knowing fine artist occur in different dialogues. A feature of Plato's epistemology is that for him knowledge of any subject requires a comprehension of opposites. He says that a man who wishes to form his judgment " . . . can no more understand earnest [drama] apart from burlesque than any other contrary apart from its contrary . . ." (*Laws* 816 D). So he concludes in the *Ion* (534 C) that poets do not do what they obviously could do if they had knowledge. They are good at treating only certain subjects; if they had knowledge, they would be expert at treating all others as well. In the early hours of the morning at the end of the *Symposium* Socrates says in a similar vein that a poet might exist who could write both tragedies and comedies. The point of his remark appears to be that there might be a philosopher-poet with the knowledge of the Forms that an ability to create opposites presupposes. The long, contrasting description by Socrates in the *Republic* of the just and unjust lives would seem to be Plato's way of showing that Socrates is, indeed, a man of just such abilities if not ambitions.

Yet Plato denies that poets and painters do portray the Forms, and he takes their inability to write both tragedies and comedies as evidence for his claim (*Republic* 395 A). He also argues that lack of knowledge is confirmed by their failure to be successful in life. Homer, for example, could never have been a successful statesman or general or businessman. That is why he merely wrote about politics and war and commerce (*Republic* 599 B). The reason for Plato's claims is clear. To admit the existence of knowledgeable artists would be to admit that the common-sense distinction between representational and nonrepresentational physical objects is incompatible with his metaphysics. The discrepancy between what occurs as an obvious possibility and what Plato denies to exist in fact has led to opposite schools of interpretation as to what his thesis is. Impressed by Plato's hostile attitude toward representational artists, Havelock denies that Plato ever suggests that poetry could constitute a likeness of a Form.[16] But Havelock is simply wrong. Even in the tenth book of the *Republic*, where the attack upon art is most heated, the question "Does the painter portray the Form Couch?" suggests that a Form for a model is a possibility. If it were not, the question would hardly arise. Then, too, the *Republic* itself is a kind of true poetry, which tries to create in words the pattern of an ideal state (*Republic* 472).

Equally impressed by the obvious possibility that a poet might represent a Form, Tate argues that Plato recognizes two kinds of art and two senses of *mimesis*: one in which a particular is the model and one in which a Form is the model. Tate admits he cannot find any such distinction in the *Republic* but remarks that at the time of writing that dialogue Plato had not yet descended to helping out mechanically minded readers by using technical terms.[17] In spite of his distaste for technical citations, Tate tries to bolster his thesis by appealing to two passages in other dialogues. At 817 B in the *Laws* Plato calls the dialogue an imitation of a noble and perfect life. Since the *Laws* is a description of a "second best" state in which law replaces reason and knowledge as sources of guidance (875 D), the most natural interpretation of this passage is that the dialogue is an imitation, not of a Form as Tate holds, but of the *Republic*, where reason instead of legislation guides the conduct of its citizens. The second passage Tate cites is one that Greene also cites to support a similar thesis.[18] At 267

16. Havelock, *Preface to Plato*, p. 37.

17. Jonathan Tate, "'Imitation' in Plato's *Republic*," *Classical Quarterly* 22 (1928): 16-23; "Plato and 'Imitation,'" *Classical Quarterly* 26 (1932): 161-69.

18. W. C. Greene, "Plato's View of Poetry," *Harvard Studies in Classical Philology* 29 (1918): 1-75.

D-E in the *Sophist* Plato distinguishes knowledgeable imitators from ignorant ones. His distinction occurs near the end of the *Sophist* as part of a final effort to define what a sophist is. The definition proceeds by distinguishing actors from painters; it then divides actors into those acquainted with the persons they mimic and those who are not. Those who mimic ignorantly do so sincerely or insincerely, and the insincere are either long- or short-winded. The sophist is a short-winded, insincere, ignorant actor (267 A-268 D).

Since the actor who "knows" his subject in these passages mimics an empirical model—another person—nothing said supports the contentions of Tate and Greene that Plato recognizes poetic imitations of the Forms. The human model the actor mimics is not for Plato a true object of knowledge; he uses the example of the mime only to illustrate the difference between what as opinion passes for knowledge—acquaintance with a particular—and total ignorance—acquaintance with nothing at all. The reason the sophist is so hard to define is that he apes the philosopher and resembles, without being, a wise man. Like Socrates, the sophist takes his form from no natural thing; his behavior is modeled on no sensory particular. Thus total ignorance and true knowledge are alike in that no objects of sensory opinion are involved. The difference between the philosopher and the sophist is that the true philosopher, Socrates, has an extrasensory set of models that guide his conduct; the sophist has none at all. Thus the philosopher is visibly like the ignorant actor who, in representing nothing at all, appears as a false philosopher. The argument of Plato is that those who haven't models for their work or conduct deserve to be called imitators, and not that those who have a set of Forms for their models are such. He does not, therefore, recognize the existence of fine artists who represent Forms, let alone of those who imitate them. Tate is quite right to point out the possibility of a painter's picturing a Form in Plato's system, but he errs in claiming that Plato admits that he exists and that he would be an imitator.

A less contentious but more peculiar claim is that of Adam, who writes of Plato as a man who didn't fully appreciate his own work and who based his condemnation of art on a narrow and scholastic interpretation of his own ontology.[19] Adam argues that a sympathetic student of Plato would find it easy to construct a nobler, more generous theory of art out of the doctrine of the Forms. He also points out, with considerable justice, that some of Plato's ideas on the possibilities of art have proved to be fountains of inspiration to Western artists. From Cicero, who aspired to be a philosopher-orator, to some of the greatest artists of the Renaissance, the attempt to portray the Forms has preoccupied a significant number of painters, poets, rhetoricians, and sculptors. Yet, the attractive possibility of a poetic picturing of a Form is an embarrassment to Plato, and he is concerned to prejudice the case of any who would claim to have realized it. If a painter really knew what he was doing, the circumstances under which he produced would turn his paintings into originals, and Plato's effort to keep a correspondence between ordinary distinctions and his philosophical theses would break down. Thus—not because of a faulty appreciation of his own work, but because of a difficulty inherent in his system—Plato engages in a polemic against all artists having the presumptuousness to claim that they know what they are doing.

The Doctrine of Divine Inspiration

The basic technique of his polemic against the poet, and its most persuasive thesis, derive from Plato's answer to still

19. Adam, *The Republic of Plato*, 2: 393.

another classificatory problem his schema presents: the problem of how to keep artifacts grouped according to the agency that produced them. In ordinary terms his problem is that of how to preserve the distinction between art and nature—a problem that differs from, but parallels that of how to preserve the sense of the distinction between models and images within the cosmos. Plato has no trouble with the originals of art and nature, since the same species of things are always designed in his view by the same agents. Man makes tools and houses, but he does not manufacture through his own, unaided efforts plants and animals. Nature raises up living creatures, but does not build the artifacts of an industrial culture. Since there are no duplicative icons, they offer no trouble either, but the imitative phantasms of the world present an important dilemma. In answering the question of where in Plato's schema an oil painting of a tree would be classed, problems arise for any reply. The painting must be of human or divine design, and so be a product of art or of nature. But such a painting does not readily fit either category. Plato's own illustrations carefully show "natural" subject matters as being portrayed by reflections or other "natural" imagery; pools of water reflect, for example, plants and animals. Likewise, the painting he mentions pictures a house which, like itself, is of human design. A discrepancy between agency and subject matter, however, poses a dilemma. The oil painting of a tree would seem, naively, to owe its origin to a human being and would seem, therefore, to be a product of art, not nature. Yet all images are identified by reference to what they are images of; two images of the same subject are identified in the same way; and in Plato's view they must be apparent members of the same class. Reflections and portraits are akin since nature, too, is art; if they represent a common, identifying model they must be disparate studies of a single subject. The oil painting of a tree and the reflections of a tree are all, for Plato, imitation trees. Thus, if one were to class the oil painting as a product of human art, a division within a single class—that of imitation trees—would arise. Consequently the distinction between art and nature would fail. Some things naturally produced would also be the fruits of artifice. Plato's difficulty, like most of those he faces, stems from his use of the circumstances of a thing's production to say what kind of thing it is.

To keep intact a correspondence between kinds of particulars and his classifications, Plato obviously must hold that the circumstances of production are always the same for each kind of thing there is. In order to establish his claim he must argue that a firm correspondence exists between the subject matter of all images and the primary agents responsible for their design. He has to hold that a divine agency predominates in the production of all images with a natural subject matter and that human agents control the production of images that imitate artificial subjects. Thus he takes what seems to be the human production of images that imitate nature to be, in reality, a form of divine art. The typical rhapsodic poet who portrays nature in verse and song creates what for Plato is a product of divine frenzy (*Ion* 533 D).

It is important to realize that Plato's doctrine of divine inspiration is integral to his analysis of the arts that imitate nature. All biologically motivated creatures seek vicarious immortality through reproduction. Poets who imitate nature share the same aim. Homer and Hesiod, for example, strove for vicarious immortality through their art (*Symposium* 209 D). Thus the needed coincidence of agency and subject matter is assured by the principle that those who imitate share in the teleology of what is imitated. Lacking knowledge, they also lack a purpose of their own. If a creative artist did not imitate nature, he would share in the teleology of what is distinctively human about us—our reason—and so would respond, like Socrates, to *thanatos* and its goal of death, rather than to *eros* and its goal of immortality. With an artificial subject matter a human telos would clearly control the mimetic act. The kind of imitation Plato discusses with approval in the early part of the *Republic* (395 C-D) is humanly inspired; so is the kind of imitation that is responsible for the second-best state described in the *Laws* (817 B; 858 C). Lodge takes the contrast between these two types of imitation to be evidence of two senses of *mimesis*; a good sense in which a Form is pictured and a bad sense in which a particular is pictured. There is, however, only one sense of *mimesis*, and the contrast Plato has in mind is not between the picturing of different levels of reality but is, instead, a contrast between different teleologies guiding the designs of poetic imagery. The unmotivated, imitative agency of the personality—the idle spirit—is clearly responsible for all imitations, but it still follows the lead of either the appetites or the reason. It is the lack of human ends in most mimetic art that Plato objects to most strongly. He accepts as useful a controlled practice of imitation responsive to the moral and intellectual interests of the soul. It is the good and wise man who is the suitable model for imitation (*Republic* 396 C-D), not nature and not the Forms.

The Polemic against the Fine Arts

The appeal to divine inspiration and the striving for vicarious immortality to explain the nature poet's work is both ingenious and convenient. It achieves the needed coincidence between agency and subject matter very plausibly in Plato's view. For him men are citizens of both culture and nature; they are supernatural souls housed in an animal body. We all, therefore, display loyalties to divine as well as human ends. Actually we are a society of agencies with our personalities divided into reasonable and appetitive parts, together with an unself-motivated spirit which, without ends of its own, follows the lead of its more determined companions. Insofar as we are animals, we respond to a divine, erotic longing for immortality—a longing that is responsible for all the cyclic processes of living nature. Thus it is difficult to tell just which actions of ours are truly human and which are divinely inspired. Whether any action or product is really human is, for Plato, open to question. Thus he can claim that the imitations of the divine order of nature are themselves of divine, not human, origin. An appeal to the ambiguity of man's motives saves the distinction between art and nature.

The attractions of the claim that nature poetry is divinely inspired are so great that they are themselves of major use to Plato. Thinking of themselves as divinely inspired delights poets such as Ion; in their delight, as well as ignorance of the implications of what they say, they are quite willing to confess to being what Plato must have them be: divine imitators whose subhuman work is done with the help, not of knowledge, but of opinion only. Their inspiration not only makes them agents of a divine teleology, but renders them incapable of explaining the meaning of their work or the principles of its construction. They do not know how to compose, but must wait upon inspiration to move them to speech (*Ion* 534 B; *Apology* 22 B-C; *Meno* 99 C; *Timaeus* 72 A). They compose, therefore, in circumstances that make their poems divine imitations. Plato uses the attractions of his thesis to get Ion to accept, unwittingly, the conclusions of the famous polemic against poets that appears in the tenth book of the *Republic*. The zeal with which not just artists but Platonic scholars have seized upon the doctrine of divine inspiration as a way to justify art provides impressive testimony on its appeal. Irked by Plato's treatment of poets, Lodge calls it an unfortunate aberration on the part of an otherwise profound intelligence and "manifestly inconsistent" with the theory of divine inspiration.[20] Verdenius also appeals to the many passages in the dialogues associating the artist with inspirational frenzy to show that Plato does have a favorable view of art.[21] Plato, however, merely uses the theory of divine inspiration to secure the coincidence between agency and subject matter that his cosmology requires. The attractions of the theory do further service, but only in securing the helpful testimony of poets that they are, as Plato's schema must have them be, ignorant and unresponsive to human values.

Plato does not patronize all inspiration. At times, for instance, he pictures his hero, Socrates, as inspired. Thus two forms of inspiration must be distinguished. When Socrates is portrayed as inspired, he is still said to be unlike the typical poet or politician in that he never writes anything—never, that is, until the last days of his life. The point Plato seems to be making about the disinterest of Socrates in writing is that he does not seek vicarious immortality through the inspired arts he practices. His source of inspiration lies beyond the world, not within it. Assured of the immortality of his soul, he has no use for a vicarious life after death such as all animals and nature poets seek. He is of no mind to leave behind him vain monuments to becoming. Plato therefore recognizes a kind of human, as well as a divine, type of inspiration. Because, however, the favorite subject matter of artists is nature—especially the instinctual actions of men under the stress of war or in the throes of

20. Lodge, *Plato's Theory of Art*, pp. 168-69.

21. W. J. Verdenius, *Mimesis: Plato's Doctrine of Artistic Imitation and its Meaning to Us* (Leiden: Brill, 1962), pp. 3-6.

passion (*Republic* 604 B-605 A)—their typical compositions are actually responsive to a divine teleology. That is the teleology which guides the natural, physiological, and instinctual processes of the body. It is in Plato's view a teleology that the reasoning soul should rule. That part of the personality, therefore, which loves nature and delights in imitating it belongs in its loyalties to the irrational, instinctual component of man in virtue of which he is an agent of nature. The susceptibility of poets to divine inspiration, far from being incompatible with their condemnation, thus becomes for Plato their basic fault. The typical poet waters the irrational appetites, establishing what ought to be ruled as the ruler in the mind. He fosters mental illness (*Republic* 605 B). The inspired nature artist, in short, is the quintessential barbarian and social misfit, unsuited to civilization. He is the unknowing doglike or horselike spirit who acts as the representative of nature inside the institutions of culture. Unfit to be raised from a state of nature, all he can do when finding himself housed against his will in a state of culture is try to revert to an irrational, unfettered existence. Accordingly, he would be banned from a well-regulated state, save for the times he might be induced to compose civilized verses obedient to a reasonable, human set of aims (*Republic* 607 A).

The harsh charges Plato brings against the rhapsodic nature poet are those his classificatory problems oblige him to bring. They are problems that suffice to explain his exclusion of nature artists from the ideal state. There is, then, absolutely no need to attempt feats of absentee psychoanalysis to explain his attitude, as Greene, Friedlander, and many other modern commentators do. Greene claims that Plato was a man "in whose own breast raged the conflict between poetry and philosophy" and whose attitude cannot be explained until his personality is.[22] Friedlander concludes that the struggle with the mimetic arts is primarily a struggle of Plato with himself.[23] Warry[24] and Crombie[25] suggest the same psychoanalytic thesis. In a similar but more fanciful vein Hack argues that Plato must have had an inordinate love of natural science and pedagogy to have banned artists from his utopia. He contrasts the unchanging laws of nature to the creative power of artists and claims that the world would be a mere mechanism without the creative power of man.[26] Hack explains that Plato thought only the laws of mechanics were real and responsible for change—a very peculiar claim to make in view of Plato's system's being the best example in Western philosophy of a teleological cosmology. The exclusion of the poets is the price Plato has to pay for interpreting the world, not as a machine, but as living, pictorial art. Equally at odds with what Plato has to say is Havelock's conclusion that Plato writes as though he had never heard of aesthetics or even of art, and in consequence insists upon treating poets as though their job is to do nothing but write metrical encyclopedias of technical and moral indoctrination.[27] For anyone to view poetry as an ineffective manual on how to produce such things as bridles and beds is, as Havelock admits, astounding. It is not, however, a view that Plato holds. The aim of the nature poet's work, he writes, is pleasure, not instruction (*Republic* 607 A; *Laws* 655 D;

22. Greene, "Plato's View of Poetry," p. 73
23. Paul Friedlander, *Plato: An Introduction* (New York: Harper and Row, 1964), p. 124.
24. J. C. Warry, *Greek Aesthetic Theory* (New York: Barnes and Noble, 1962), p. 55.
25. Crombie, *An Examination of Plato's Doctrines*, 1: 195.
26. R. K. Hack, "The Doctrine of Literary Forms," *Harvard Studies in Classical Philology* 27 (1916): 1-66.
27. Havelock, *Preface to Plato*, pp. 29-30.

Statesman 288 C; *Gorgias* 502 C). What Plato writes about art is not a function of ignorance or neurotic self-division; it is a function of what he takes the world to be like, and nothing else. His metaphysics, his epistemology, and his psychology come together to form an integrated poetics, the parts of which are to be explained by principles internal to his philosophical system.

The strands of ambition and thought that tie together Plato's remarks about the arts also give cohesion to his political doctrines. His polemical attack on the nature artist is but one aspect, indeed, of a more general denunciation of a traditional cultural and political order to which the utopian vision of the *Republic* stands in contrast. Plato draws a parallel between poets and political leaders whom he feels obliged to attack. He compares the lawmaker Solon, for example, to Homer (*Symposium* 209 D). In contrast, he compares his theoretical philosopher-king to industrial artisans (*Statesman* 260 A) and to animal breeders (*Republic* 459 B). Clearly, there is a way in which the notions of imitating, adding, and aiding apply to political theory. I now want to examine what that way is.

5

Politics–The Human Alliance of Reason and Knowledge

The Parallel between Poets and Politicians

Plato's comparison of Solon to Homer is not the only case of his grouping a lawmaker with an artist. He thinks Lycurgus was somehow like Hesiod. He also describes Themistocles, Aristides, Pericles, and Thucydides in terms that match his description of the poet Ion. Important arguments in the *Republic*, the *Meno*, the *Phaedrus*, the *Apology*, the *Laws*, and the *Symposium* link political to aesthetic analysis. In Plato's view the aesthetic configuration of a society is symptomatic of its political bias. The kind of arts and the kind of artists that a given city honors indicate what kind of laws and what kind of leaders it has. The poets and politicians of Athens, for example, are the natural allies and mutual supporters of each other. Anyone who would try to reform Athenian society must expect the opposition of both groups—a lesson Socrates learned at the cost of his life (*Apology* 22 A-C). Anyone, too, who would merely discuss how a truly just state might be created must recognize the need to banish or control all poets (*Republic* 606 E-607 A). A new political order will inevitably mean a new aesthetic order (*Laws* 817 A-E). Plato's indictment of the art of his age is clearly only a part of a larger indictment he brings against the laws and institutions of a society he regards as somehow akin to the poetry of the irrational rhapsodist.

When contemplating the link between Plato's attack on poetry and his demands for the reform of Athenian political life, one may—as many have done—put his views down to simple paranoia, or zealotry, or a totalitarian's fear of free expression. But the matter goes deeper than any psychological trait Plato may have had. The interweaving of aesthetic and political analysis forms an argumentative design whose most basic motifs display the structural principles of his philosophy. All change is a form of artistic, pictorial creativity. Any social change—including the passing of old institutions, laws, and styles of life, or the coming of new ones—is therefore a product of art. It is not just astronomy, biology, and carpentry that Plato tries to understand in terms of portraiture, but the fields of politics and jurisprudence as well. Indeed, one of his prime motives for arguing that the cosmos is divine art is to enable him to say that the legal and social conventions of man are of no different standing than the derivative artificialities of "nature." Lawmaking, like everything else, is an artist's enterprise. Thus Plato compares, favorably, his own efforts to write political philosophy to the efforts of painters (*Republic* 472 C-D), playwrights, and poets (*Laws* 817 B) to draw pictures and compose dramas and verses. A similar comparison must be in order when analyzing the work of other men who have either written law codes or have had an influence on the design of the political and social institutions of a city. Not all comparisons will be the same, of course; change may always be the product of art; but, depending on the circumstances under which one creates, there are different kinds of art. One may add to the world, aid it, or imitate it. Plato weaves together his attack on poetry with his attack on Athenian political life because he sees both traditional poets and traditional politicians as imitators of the order of nature. In their case aesthetic and political analyses go hand in hand because they share the same subhuman teleology and the same lamentable lack of knowledge. They are natural allies because they are committed to creating their poems and law codes under exactly the same circumstances. Artists are not, then, a danger to justice simply because of their outspoken, undisciplined ways; they are dangerous because the principles of their art may easily spread to the body politic, with the result that culture itself becomes a mere imitation of the incomplete and botched organic nature it ought to add to and aid. In Plato's judgment Athenian culture is all too much like the rhapsodic nature poetry it honors. Any effort to reform it must begin by restricting the influence of that mob of imitators which, up until now, has made its popular art, designed its basic institutions, and held its highest offices.

Numerous passages indicate that Plato does, indeed, view the typical poet and the typical politician as two of a kind. Both, he claims, respond to the divine teleology of nature. Solon and Lycurgus sought vicarious immortality for themselves through their law codes in the same way that nature poets have done through their verses (*Symposium* 209 D; *Phaedrus* 258 C). Poets and politicians are also men who lack knowledge. Just as Homer lacked the ability to educate men (*Republic* 600 C-E), so the typical political leader is unable to communicate his skills to anyone else (*Apology* 21 C; *Meno* 93 E - 94 D). Since a true, teachable art requires knowledge, whereas a mere empirical knack that cannot be taught is based on opinion (*Meno* 98 D), politicians in Plato's judgment are without knowledge. Thus the analysis of the divinely inspired poet in the *Ion* applies equally to the traditional politician. He is like a prophet or oracle who may utter many apparent truths, but without having knowledge of what he is saying, speaking as he does while divinely inspired (*Meno* 99 B-D; *Phaedrus* 278 B-C).

The two respects in which the typical poet and the typical lawmaker are alike fix, of course, the ontological and teleological circumstances under which they produce their poems and law codes. Lacking knowledge, they create artifacts that are imitations, not originals. Responding to the teleology of nature, they create artifacts that are really of divine, not human, design. Thus the typical lawmaker, like the typical poet, is to be associated with the idle, imitative, and unknowing spirit in the personality. The laws and institutions he designs, like landscape paintings, are also to be classed as belonging to the defective, incomplete order of nature. Like the poet, the politician is the quintessential barbarian and social misfit, unsuited to civilization. He may appear to be an upholder of culture, but actually he is a man who, in his devotion to nature and its ways, can neither add to nor aid the world. Consequently, he is not a man with either the loyalties or the knowledge a true culture requires of its citizens.

The polemical broadcasting of these sentiments would appear to be the cause of Socrates' indictment, trial, and execution by Athenian authorities. It was men aggrieved on behalf of poets, politicians, and kindred professionals who brought charges against him (*Apology* 23 E; *Republic* 473 E - 474 A). And well they might have felt aggrieved. The position of Socrates - and that of Plato - amount to a condemnation of virtually the whole of Greek political and artistic history. The laws and institutions of Athens are as far removed in Plato's judgment from the truth as the images of art are. They are also equally responsive to biological, subhuman, instinctual ends. They must, therefore, promote the same injustice and illnesses in the mind and society that poetry does. In excluding the nature poet from their vision of an ideal state, Socrates and Plato are also arguing that the typical political leader and lawmaker should join the artist in exile as a danger to the well-being of those he has led. He, too, is an ignorant barbarian of the spirit, unfit for life in a civilized setting.

The teleological component of Plato's attack upon the likes of Solon, Lycurgus, and Pericles is immediately clear. They are simply participants in the defective, biological teleology of nature that seeks to continue life without adding to or improving it. The doctrine that the laws and institutions they have designed are imitations of nature, however, is harder to grasp. To see what Plato means, it is necessary to understand that he adopts a representational theory of culture. He describes most traditional laws and institutions as somehow reflecting aspects of nature. What he seems to have in mind is that a person's biological traits will often fix his rights and his social position. Being male gives him certain privileges as well as responsibilities as the legal head of a household. Being Greek establishes other rights and responsibilities. Birth and kinship relations also affect his legal and social standing, often determining such important matters as his claims to citizenship, to enfranchisement, to inherited property, to class, to profession, and even to office. Sex, race, parentage, and blood kinship thus are profoundly important in assessing social position. But the basis of the assessment has only to do with one's biological, natural traits and relations. It would seem to be that fact which makes Plato describe certain traditional laws and institutions as imitations of nature. One's social standing, his point is, reflects one's biological status. The designers of traditional codes and traditional institutions have, in his judgment, looked to biological marks and relations to guide them in their work. Thus they are like painters and poets who have designed their poems and pictures as representations of an organic, subhuman world. Greek culture is analogous to Greek art. The same basic principles of design and teleology are present in each. That fact is clearly the reason why any true political reformer would give a high priority to rooting out of the state its poets. Their work is emblematic of an ethos that pervades the entire social order. As long as they are allowed to continue their work, a true code of law and of reason will never be lord of the city (*Republic* 607 A), for the city's laws will be but imitations of an irrationally designed nature. The attack upon art is the theoretical equivalent of the *Republic's* call for political and social reform.

The basic example of an institution that fits Plato's political analysis is the family. It is an institution that obviously serves the interests of specific preservation through the begetting and rearing of children. It is, then, an institution easily thought of as responsive to the organic teleology of nature. The social relations internal to the family just as obviously reflect biological relations. Titles such as "mother," "father," "son," "uncle," and so on are social titles that carry with them certain rights and responsibilities. But they are also, first and foremost, biological titles. It is, for example, only by virtue of his biological relations that a father acquires moral and legal authority over his son. Thus his authority rests on a biological trait, and one could say with Plato that the social structure of familial authority represents a biological structure. So, in both aim and model, the family stands as the prime example of an institution whose origin requires that it be classified as a divine imitation. The more general theory that virtually the whole political structure of the traditional state is to be classified in the same way amounts to the thought that the state is a kind of family writ large—a kinship grouping devoted to the preservation of life and with lines of authority resting on claims of biological hegemony.

Given the tenacity with which Plato draws his analogy between poets and politicians, it is clear that his critique of traditional law and culture rests on the point that a way of life following a creed of men with the commitments of Solon, Pericles, and Lycurgus is politically a derivative version of the order of nature. His point provides him with a key forensic reply to the extreme moral skeptics and political nihilists of his day who equated justice with conformity to natural law. In the *Gorgias* (483 C-E) the sophist Callicles declares that the true character of right lies in acting in accord with nature's own law—a law of survival for the fit and the selfish—and that anyone who is sufficiently strong will shake loose from the egalitarian fetters of convention, which presently enslave the best among us, to rise up as our master in the manner of the tyrant. Plato's implicit rejoinder to Callicles' call in the name of natural right for a revolution of the strong against the weak is that in important respects traditional society is aligned in both model and agency with the order of "nature." Its laws and its aims derive mainly from biological relations and impulses. It already is, in major ways, the "natural" society that Callicles calls for. But that is precisely what is wrong with it. The principle that the natural and the just are associated is legitimate, but only when "nature" is used in an accurate way. The Forms, as Nature, do provide ultimate standards of right conduct. Because the soul can assimilate itself to the Forms by imitating them, it, too, might become natural to the extent permitted to man (*Republic* 500 C-D). A city participating directly in a pattern provided by the Forms—reflecting them more completely and more clearly than the plant and animal kingdoms do—and responding to the soul's aspirations, could also be described as a city wherein everyone is ruled by a principle of natural justice (*Republic* 456 C). If, however, it is the divine but incomplete and imperfect art Callicles erronously calls nature that is the pattern for a city's laws, and the bodily appetites provide their telos, then that city must be considered artificial. It would not correct matters in any way to abandon reason and law altogether and allow the city to be ruled by Callicles' unprincipled tyrant in whom the unfettered, selfish appetites hold sway. In that case the city would lose whatever affinity to the Forms it might have and simply become nothing less than a functioning part of divine art, as far removed as possible from the love of law and order, which are the prime marks of everything aspiring to the truly natural (*Republic* 587 A-B). The proposals of Callicles and others of his persuasion, such as Antiphon, amount to proposals for transforming traditional society into an even more, not less, conventional, unnatural realm than it already is. Thus Plato succeeds in retaining the association of the natural with the just, while escaping the conclusion that we should return to an uncivilized state of nature dominated by the totally savage. We can, his point is, approximate a true state of Nature, or *physis*, in our lives only by refusing to return to nature, so called, and by refusing to imitate the irrational, botched art that composes it. The metaphysical equation of appearance with art is obviously of major polemical use in allowing him to reply to the moral and political nihilists of his day. He accepts their principle that the natural is the right, but only to use it against them. If one wants to build a more natural city than Athens presently is, then one will have to increase, not lessen, the restraints placed on self-interest and animal inclination.

Plato's attack on Athenian culture does not, of course, exhaust itself in the forensic point that, by being imitative of what we call nature, traditional law is really artificial. That point is but the start of a detailed indictment of traditional society. His basic, substantive complaint is that the mentally ill have designed and ruled the Greek city-state. The basis of his complaint is the observation that the idle, imitative spirit has dominated the work of the traditional politician. The only two agencies of the mind capable of true teleological leadership, however, are the reason and the appetites. The appetites would govern us in a pure state of nature, so called; short of living in such a state—which would be thoroughly impractical as well as unjust—another agency must be held responsible for our laws and institutions. Because the structure of traditional society is largely imitative of nature, the conclusion must be drawn that the idle spirit has inappropriately revolted to assume in the life of Solon, Pericles, and other lawmakers a ruling position it does not deserve. Its nature is such that it ought always to serve as a slave to a ruling agency (*Republic* 444 B). As a result of its revolt, a kind of civil war of the mind has characterized the traditional political leader, and his work must be considered symptomatic of mental derangement. Because justice simply is minding one's own business and doing one's own work in the matter of ruling and being ruled (*Republic* 443 B), Plato condemns as unjust as well as sick the mentality of a man in whom the spirit assumes dominance. Indeed, his argument is that mental pathology is indistinguishable from injustice. Thus, by allowing a principle with no right to rule to assume hegemony in his personality, the traditional political leader is rendered unfit on both moral and medicinal grounds to govern others.

The sickly, unjust cast of the typical lawmaker's personality reflects itself in the social order he directs. He encourages the rebellion of the spirit in everyone, thereby turning them into strife-ridden neurotics like himself. He also organizes the relations between people in such a way that they often do not do the work they are best suited to do, thereby violating the basic precept of justice. The reason he is such a poor administrator is that, being essentially an imitative type, he mimics in law the order of nature. By using nature, so called, as his guide he is bound to exclude from his work any major consideration of what a person is best suited to do. A community of human beings should, obviously, be designed to fulfill the ambitions and meet the needs of human beings. In the assignment of their social duties to people, a high priority should therefore be placed on their human qualities. But what is human about a person has nothing to do with biology. It is the inorganic soul—the moral and intellectual faculties—that is human. Ancestry, kinship, sex, and race are improper criteria to use in assigning to a person his or her social position. When they are used, people will often be placed in inappropriate classes, inappropriate professions, and inappropriate offices. Those fit to rule, for example, have invariably been the ruled in Plato's judgment, not the rulers. Thus, in a social order that imitates nature, people will often not do the work their truly human capacities qualify them to do. The principle that justice is everyone's minding his own business and doing his own work is bound to be violated. The mental pathology of a state's imitative leaders must, Plato concludes, result in social pathology. With that conclusion in mind, he insists in the *Republic* on examining strife and injustice in the personality before defining strife and injustice in the state. One can best understand a thing when one understands its cause, and the etiology of social injustice lies in the field of mental pathology.

Aside from indicting traditional society as pathologically unjust, Plato condemns it as restricting the soul's freedom. It is comparable to the jail house of the body and to the cavernous dungeon of the world itself. During the course of the conversations that the *Crito* and *Phaedo* record, a strong analogy is drawn between the stones of the prison in which Socrates is kept during the last days of his life and the flesh that surrounds his soul. Gradually it becomes clear, however, that the prison stands as well for the whole makeup of Athenian civilization, which has, throughout his life, imprisoned Socrates in the fetters of uncongenial institutions. His city has been a second jail, surrounding the first, which is his body. In good humor he calls his flesh a place of protective custody for his soul and rejects the suggestion that he has the right to depart life in suicide before his heavenly jailers release him. Likewise, in equally good humor, he refuses to consider escape from his earthly guards. In his view the laws of the city that has nurtured him as a mother would her child, are akin to the laws of a parent (*Crito* 51 B), and to them he feels an onerous, but binding obligation. Athens has always been for him a place of protective custody—a city-prison that responds to a defective, subhuman teleology and that imitates in its political dimensions the botched, incomplete art of the plant and animal kingdoms. Yet he will not break the laws of its officials. Neither will he disobey the divinities who have placed him in his body. To his original jailers and their imitators he will remain loyal to the end—even though he is happy enough for the chance to escape both at last through the legal expedient of drinking his hemlock.

There have been few, if any, social critics who have been harder on their cities than Socrates and Plato were on Athens. Yet, like most who take the trouble to criticize their homes, these men temper their polemics with affection, even admiration, for what they indict. Plato is careful to mute his attack on Athenian life with a qualification and several acts of contrition. He also offers a flattering recipe for how matters might possibly be righted. Although the divine art of nature is a savage realm, he refuses to think of it as evil. Neither does he regard as evil the poems and laws that imitate it. After making light of the divine power of love in the *Phaedrus*, Socrates is bothered by feelings of guilt, and he repents of his impiety by delivering a speech praising Eros in all its forms (242 E). His attitude toward the imitations of love's originals is similar. He attacks the fine arts vehemently, but eventually he purges himself of the disrespect he has shown them by writing poetry at the end of his life in the *Phaedo*. In parallel fashion, he acknowledges that the laws of Athens deserve respect (*Crito* 52 D). Although products of opinion, not knowledge, they still suffice for many purposes (*Meno* 97 C). His imprisonment in Athens, he carefully notes, is benign, not malevolent. The trouble with a culture that imitates nature is not, then, that it is evil or contemptible. The trouble is only that in it a derangement of essentially good and proper principles has occurred. With a sound reordering of those principles, any objection voiced by Socrates against their designs would be met. What is needed is someone to duplicate in the political life of man the work done by the *demiourgos* when he brought the stars from disorder into order. Athens, with all its men of expert knowledge, might supply that someone. He would be a philosopher-king. If a true philosopher would only combine his knowledge with political power, then the institutions of Athens could be redesigned and injustice and strife could be eliminated from both the personality and the social order. What is already fair and grand in the city would then find a fuller, even nobler expression. Its dormant greatness, of which there is much evidence, would be wakened.

Philosophy and the Human Control of Culture

The philosopher would be the rightful ruler of Plato's utopia because he is the only person in whom a proper ordering of the agencies of the personality can be found. His soul, or reason, controls both the appetites and the spirit. He spends his life rehearsing death, and so is quite unlike all those who work only in the hope of a vicarious immortality. Nature's irrational, erotic goals are not his own. His personality is analogous to a well-driven chariot whose horses respond in tandem to the responsible, thanatological goals of its driver. The state he might come to rule would share in the same analogy. It is, of course, crucially important for the reason to control both the mind and the state, because it is the only agency competent to do so. The teleology of the appetites is defective and would, at best, be an appropriate guide for biological organisms in a pure state of nature. Since we are not mere animals, and couldn't live for long anyway without some form of organized political and social life, the appetites are fundamentally unqualified to lead us—a lesson that any tyranny, in which the appetites reign unchecked, would teach to anyone with the courage to learn and the luck to survive. The spirit, in turn, is without a teleology of its own; thus it cannot rule without disturbing the structure of both the mind and the state. The reason is left as the only agency fit to rule.

The clarity of the right of the reason to rule raises the question of why it is so seldom exercised. Few men, in Plato's judgment, are actually healthy and no state has ever been. A partial explanation for this sorry state of affairs is, says Socrates, that no champion of justice could survive with his life for long in politics (*Apology* 32 A). Cities kill their most reasonable citizens. It is no wonder, then, that there are few who might bring justice to the state. But a fuller explanation lies in Plato's psychological theory. What qualifies the reason to hold high office is also what will often prevent it from assuming high office. The reason is the carrier of the rational teleology of appearance. That is its prime psychological and political credential. When it directs the change characteristic of appearance, it strives to make particulars as full participants in reality as possible. It improves the world by giving to change a goal beyond itself. But in order to carry out its function, the reason must love the Forms and appreciate their features more than it loves or appreciates the conceptually defective features of particulars. Its thanatological loyalties are essential to its role as the carrier of a rational teleology in which means and ends, becoming and being, are kept distinct; but those loyalties are apt to render it indifferent to the world. It may simply seek the death of the body so as to return to the Forms, which it can only recollect, not contemplate, on earth. Men in whose personalities the reason rules make, indeed, dying their profession (*Phaedo* 67 E). They never want to occupy themselves with the affairs of men, but always feel an urge to sojourn above the cavernous art of their world (*Republic* 517 C). It is no surprise, then, that politicians, in whom the unqualified spirit prevails, have gained control of the state. They have become leaders, not so much by overt rebellion, as by simple default. They, at least, love appearance and delight in the conception and generation of change that are proper to it. They will take pains to bind together a society in fetters of love to insure that something even lovelier and less mortal than human seed will survive forever in space and time (*Symposium* 209 C). Competence to rule and ambition to rule thus seldom coincide. That is the real explanation for why neurotic strife and injustice prevail in the affairs of men. That is why, too, they may always prevail. If matters are ever to right themselves, those competent to rule must either be compelled to do so (*Republic* 519 D-E) or must, by chance, be born to binding responsibilities of office they cannot escape (*Republic* 502 A). Whether either condition will ever be met is a question only history can decide.

Even though no philosopher may ever assume power, his policies and the broad outlines of the state he would design are clear. A philosopher-king, Socrates says, would begin his reign by rusticating the population of his city over ten years of age. The remainder he would treat as plastic material from which he would fashion living representations of all the virtues and all the various pursuits of men (*Republic* 500 D). To achieve his ends he would work like an ordinary sculptor or painter, except that his materials and his models and his purpose would differ. He would use living creatures instead of clay or pigment, and he would take care to pattern his work on the unseen Forms and the structure of the mind itself, not the botched, empirical bodies of those he has rusticated. He would also make no effort to immortalize himself through his work, but rather merely try to fashion his populace into as full likenesses of the Forms he loves as possible. As a kind of political artisan of human character he would function as a creator capable of ontologically adding to appearance, and he would provide his handiwork with a human, rational teleology. He would thus stand in contrast to the typical politician as the industrial artisan and the informed animal breeder stand in contrast to the typical painter and the quack doctor.

The ties of the philosopher-reformer to the circumstances of production that fix the manufacture of humanly designed originals determines the basic features of the state he would create. A prime concern of his would be to guarantee the social and political hegemony of a truly human teleology. That guarantee would be provided by a system of education and psychiatric testing designed to discover the dominant features of a child's personality. If its reason were found to prevail over its appetites and its spirit, it would be assigned to a ruling class of administrators. If the spirit showed signs of dominating, the child would be placed in an auxiliary class of soldier-guardians under the strict supervision of civilian administrators. If the appetites were obviously in control, the child would end up in a third class of artisans and farmers. In this way the social structure of the state would be made responsive to human, not divine, aspirations and needs. The true teleology of appearance would inform the city; and from a prison it would be changed into a temporary, congenial home of the soul's own making.

Because a prime objective of a human, rational teleology is to make appearances participate as far as possible in the superior features of reality, another major concern of the philosopher-reformer would be to breed from his populace a superior race. He would probably not be able to succeed with all people (*Republic* 457 E), but it should be possible for him to use his ruling administrators as breeding stock, obedient as they are to the goals of reason. It should be possible, too, for him to use his auxiliary guardians, since they are prepared to imitate the behavior of the fully reasonable (*Republic* 458 C). The philosopher-reformer would intervene in the reproductive efforts of both these classes by getting the best men to cohabit with the best women. The worst men would be left to cohabit with the worst women, but if born defective, their offspring would be purged in secret to preserve the purity and clarity of the breed (*Republic* 460 A-C). The result would be an ever-closer approximation of the human body to the features of the Forms it participates in. The celestial work of the *demiourgos* would be duplicated in the case of man by man himself.

In the event that the philosopher-reformer breeds a superior race, a distinctively human teleology would come to the aid of nature. A thanatological impulse would cooperate with *eros* to give the reproductive process a goal beyond itself. What is human and what is divine about us would then work in harmony. Consequently, the most important source of mental conflict in man would disappear. By raising the work of *eros* to meet the true, thanatological goals of appearance, the philosopher-reformer would finally eliminate from the personality and the state the strife Plato equates with injustice. Thus there is a link between Plato's theory of justice and his teleology. The reason, as the keeper of the world's true ambitions, is the rightful ruler of both the personality and the state because, in implementing its policies, it automatically brings to a close the civil conflicts that constitute injustice. The just state and the just mind are necessarily responsive to the authority of what is human in us. By moving to guarantee the hegemony of a human teleology, the philosopher-reformer would move to create, not merely a social order in which the soul would feel at home, but a healthy and fair one as well. Freedom, health, and justice all depend on the city's allegiance to the true, rational telos of change. If Athens could be brought to align itself fully with that telos, all its present defects would be corrected.

Aside from its teleological peculiarities, a reformed Athens would adopt novel institutions. None of them would be an imitation of some aspect of organic nature. Neither would any be modeled on Forms that nature itself participates in. They all would be full additions to the world in the double ontological and teleological senses of representing the Forms directly and of having no counterparts in the rival realm of nature's divine art. No citizen, for example, would inherit his social position. Parentage would determine neither occupation nor class (*Republic* 415 C). Sex, too, would cease to be a way of fixing a person's status and duties. Women would have to participate in military campaigns, hunting, and field work. They would also be members of the ruling administrators. In all other respects they would be considered the equal of men, save in the single point of strength (*Republic* 451 E). Indeed, the family itself would disappear in the ruling classes of the utopian state. The social relations between guardians and administrators would not reflect biological relations. The state would raise children in ignorance of who their parents and blood kin are. The result would be a severe limitation on the biological significance of such titles as "brother," "sister," "mother," and "father." Kinship would cease to figure in even the meaning of these words. No matter whom a child meets, he would be taught to feel that he is meeting a brother, a sister, a mother, a father, or some other kin (*Republic* 463 C). A similar prohibition on the use of racial criteria to fix social status would be enforced, it seems fair to say, if racial differences existed in the city's population. The constant point Plato makes is that a utopian statesman would assign to the same natures the same pursuits (*Republic* 456 B). He would use, not the biological differentia of the world's divine art, but the unseen qualities of the personality to fix a person's social position. Since the personality is nothing empirical, and at least the reasoning agency can mingle with the *physis* of the Forms, it is possible for it to imitate reality and so assimilate itself to what is truly natural (*Republic* 500 C). Thus, in a largely forensic sense, the utopian city would be a natural city. That sense requires that in model, as well as in agency, it remain distinct from divine conventions. Actually, in normal terms—where birth, sex, race, and kinship are taken to be natural properties and relations—the *Republic* is the great portrait in Western philosophy of a thoroughly artificial society. Its utopia, like Socrates, would take its form from no natural thing.

In spite of the strong differences Plato draws between the traditional Greek city-state and his utopian society, it is clear that his attitude reflects the bias of his form of civilization and that he is, in fact, defending what is most distinctive about it. The form that civilization took in classical antiquity was the urban life of the city-state; and the contrast Plato draws between human and divine art is, in his view, basically a contrast between urban civilization and rural barbarism. One reason that he eventually became the most important philosopher of antiquity is that his theories act as an explanation, as well as a justification, for its form of life. There is in the dialogues a more or less constant view expressed that all beyond the walls of the city is barbarism. The spirits of rural haunts are comparable to dogs, sheep, and horses, which must, even for their own good, be trained in obedience to man. Nature itself is incomplete, botched, and in need of aid. Plato's attack upon the traditional institutions of Athenian culture rests on the point that they are too infected with the faulty aspirations of nature. His vision of an ideal commonwealth is a vision of a true city in which the reasoning soul controls the barbarism of instinct and impulse. His critique of his civilization is in this respect clearly a function of his defense of what is most distinctive about it. He portrays Socrates, for example, as a martyr, whose unjust death of the hands of his fellow citizens is a judgment against them and their laws. But at the same time Plato presents Socrates as the most representative man of the civilization that condemned him. He is the quintessential city dweller, the oddest of men, according to Phaedrus, who never so much as sets foot outside the walls of Athens (*Phaedrus* 230 C-D).

The portrait of Socrates as an urban guru—quite uncomfortable in the usual haunts of the wise man in forest hut or cave—serves as an important part of Plato's justification of what he took civilization to be. Unlike the philosopher Aristippus, who abandoned civilization for the wilds of North

Africa, or the philosopher Diogenes, who tried to live in accord with nature in his barrel in downtown Corinth, Socrates professes to be at home only within the walls of his city. He seems committed instinctively to the tasks of culture, and he argues that it is the height of perversity for man to ape the rival ways of nature. His view in no way precludes all criticism of the city-state, of course, for Plato judges the culture of his day as harshly as any of the sophist-philosophers he opposes. His judgment, however, is quite unlike that of the typical sophist such as Diogenes; rather than criticize his culture as the unnatural construction of man, he condemns it for not being "unnatural" enough. Too many of its institutions, he argues, embody the uncivilized, defective aspirations of nature, and so fail to reflect the interests of what is truly human about us. In his view the Athenian state is defective, not because it is a city, but because the frenzied art of nature infects it. The broad outlines of the *Republic's* utopian vision are, then, related to the features of Athenian society in a way analogous to the way a human teleology is related to a divine teleology. It is an improved, fuller version of the artificial, cultural setting man has designed for himself. The legal and institutional respects in which Athens is imitative of nature are really anomalies, pervasive as they are, for they are out of character with the urban, industrial life they regulate. They conflict with what is most distinctive about the state, blurring its supra-organic structure and bringing to its citizenry psychic discord. What Socrates asks of his fellow Athenians is that they be fully and consistently what they basically are: urban men and women who, in being supernatural, have added a noble art of their own to the world in the form of the city they have built. Their additions are not yet complete, for a fully civilized setting would require their abandoning imitative political institutions. They should match with their architecture and their industry and their animal breeding their social and legal institutions. To do that they should find someone to rule as capable of perfecting their human and social qualities as the animal trainer is capable of perfecting the natural qualities of colts and calves (*Apology* 20 A-B). If and when such a person is ever found, the implicit program of Athenian culture will be complete. Thus Socrates, for all his indictments of poets and politicians, is really a gadfly, urging his fellow citizens on to do what they are already doing, and to complete the work of civilization and the ascent from nature they have begun. He is, if they only understood, even more their defender than he is their critic. He is the anti-sophist who would protect them from the denigration of their style of civilization. His arguments are designed to sanction their urban form of life, and his just republic is nothing but their Athens made consistent.

The Second-Best Society and Plato's Classification of the Political Arts

Plato is acutely sensitive to the point that a utopian society would be difficult to achieve. He has little confidence that it ever will be. Reason, in the form of the true philosopher, has never ruled a society. Except for lawless eras of utter savagery, when the appetites, in the form of the tyrant, have ruled supreme in what amounts to a full state of nature, it has always been the spirit, in the form of the traditional lawmaker, that has governed. Accordingly, the lessons of history suggest that the only practical program of social reform would center on getting the actual holders of political power to change their allegiances. The social order is likely to remain a product of spirited imitation. Imitators, however, have no teleology of their own, and it is conceivable that they might turn from their traditional mimicking of nature to model their work on a utopian pattern. They haven't done this in the past, of course, but that is perhaps because no such pattern has been available to them and their ignorance renders them incapable of supplying their own. As a piece of literary exposition, the *Republic* is not a functioning state that represents the Forms directly. Still, it is a product of reason, and it does portray the Forms in the medium of language. It is, indeed, comparable to the work of a poet or painter who pictures, not appearances, but an ideal (*Republic* 472 D). It is thus a kind of literary equivalent to a functioning, utopian society, and it could be used as the empirical model the imitative politician needs to create his laws. That the *Republic* should serve as a guide to the imitative lawmaker would seem to be one of the purposes Plato had in mind in writing it, for he disavows any intent of demonstrating the possibility of the ideals he discusses (*Republic* 472 C). He appears to offer his dialogue simply as an empirical pattern for legislators to imitate. If those with power were to imitate it, a state most nearly answering to the description of a utopia would result, and with the realization of that second-best possibility he would be content (*Republic* 473 A-B). Of all the disorder in the world, that endemic to man's own affairs is the most difficult to eradicate. The most that can be expected is an imitation of what would be best.

The *Laws* is an examination of what a state would be like that imitated the institutions described in the *Republic* (*Laws* 739 D-E). One of the outstanding features of such a state would be that legislation, not the dictates of reason, would guide decision-makers (*Laws* 875 C). It would be a constitutional state. The explanation for why a constitution would be needed lies in the governing presumption of the dialogue; any second-best state would be regulated, Plato presumes, by right opinion, not knowledge; and one of the marks of a person with opinions only is that, like a cook or apprentice doctor, he must look up in a manual what it would be best for him to do. Legislation is the manual of the administrator who lacks knowledge. What he finds out from his reading can at best be right opinion, of course, since otherwise he would acquire knowledge, and that would violate the basic precept that only the Forms can be sources of knowledge. Since Plato associates opinion with the production of imitations, the society the *Laws* describes is clearly the product of unknowing imitators. Its ruling principle is the spirited part of the personality, and its features reflect, not reality, but mere appearances.

Because of the lack of knowledge on the part of the state's administrators, Plato argues that a system of censorship and thought control would be essential to the government. Opinions, falling short as they do of the truth, cannot be demonstrated. They are likely stories at best. That they are merely stories is apparently the reason why the skills and virtues of those possessing opinion only cannot, in Plato's judgment, be taught. One can't teach what one does not know and cannot demonstrate, but opinions can neither be known nor be demonstrated. Therefore opinion cannot be taught. Persuasion is for this reason of limited use to the state if confined to rational argument. State administrators would be profoundly concerned with empirical, practically useful forms of instruction, but they would be incapable of teaching anything scientifically. In order to get people to believe tenets crucial to their own well-being and to the authority of the state, it would be necessary to reinforce probable arguments and likely pleas with censorship and an enforced code of orthodoxy, or right opinion (*Laws* 801 D;

829 D; 886 D.). The state's code of prescribed conviction would function as an important part of its program to imitate the educational curriculum of the *Republic*.

The imitative, unknowing character of the society the *Laws* describes makes it, of course, akin to the traditional society of Solon, Pericles, and the other lawmakers Plato attacks for their want of knowledge. The censorship, however, does not extend to a commonality of either models or teleology. In these two respects a fundamental contrast exists. Whereas traditional law is an imitation of nature and is responsive to a divine telos, the whole polity of the *Laws* is an imitation, a drama, of a noble and perfect life of utopian culture and is responsive to a human telos. Thus its leaders are like traditional poets and politicians in that they work in the same manner, but they remain rival artists, rival poets, and rival dramatists (*Laws* 817 B). They do not respond to the muses of nature, and their work is therefore incompatible with the compositions of traditional art and politics. The rhapsodic poets attacked in the *Republic* and the kindred politicians attacked in the *Meno* are still excluded from the polity of the *Laws*.

The teleology of the legislators in charge of the second-best state would commit them to a program of racial improvement. It could not be so ambitious a program as that of the *Republic*, for marriage would have to be allowed, and the ill and botched could not be purged all at once. In place of rusticating the old and recalcitrant, legislators could send away the worst to colonies, keeping the best as a kind of stock from which a still better citizenry might emerge (*Laws* 735E-736A). Likewise, the pattern adopted as a model for legislation would require that biological criteria be abandoned as far as possible in assigning social positions. The family would remain the basic social unit, but rights of inheritance would be severely limited (*Laws* 923 A), and children would be freely distributed among the households of the state to insure a uniformity of population (*Laws* 740 B-D). Education and all institutions would be devised for both sexes alike (*Laws* 781 B; 765 D). Thus the principles of the *Republic* would be retained insofar as is practicable. The state would be an imitative order, ruled by the unknowing, but it would not be dominated by the desire to achieve only a vicarious form of immortality, and it would not ape in its institutions, any more than it had to, the rival ways of nature. It would thus differ profoundly from the traditional state, in spite of its leaders' lack of knowledge.

Given the marked differences between the kinds of society Plato recognizes as theoretical possibilities, and given as well the affinities between his views on politics, art, and psychology, a classification revealing the structural coherence of his doctrines on all these topics could be made as follows:

HUMAN		DIVINE		
Utopia (Philosophers as rulers)	Industrial Art (Industrial Artisans as creators)	State of Nature (Tyrants as rulers)	Animals (Parents as creators)	ORIGINALS
Second-Best State (Legislative Imitators as rulers)	Rational Art (Artistic Imitators of the good and the wise as creators)	Traditional State (Legislative Imitators of nature as creators)	Rhapsodic Art (Artistic Imitators of nature as creators)	IMITATIONS

Plato's Critics and Defenders

The coherence of Plato's political views and their links with his psychological, epistemological, and metaphysical doctrines makes it clear that what he says about politics is as much a function of his theories about man and the world as his aesthetic dicta are. An appreciation of this point may help resolve a dispute about his political stand that has gone on for years among his detractors and defenders, many of whom have failed to recognize his motives and have not sufficiently appreciated the highly theoretical cast of his doctrines.

Karl Popper has argued with great heat that Plato was a totalitarian political theorist whose utopia was based on an ethnic racist "naturalism," a disregard for individuality, and a fanatical faith in his own vision of truth.[1] The opposition in Plato's cosmology between the Forms and particulars manifests itself, Popper claims, in the priority Plato gives to the collective state over the individuals who make it up. The state's political tyranny is then justified, Popper concludes, by an appeal to theories of "biological naturalism," which glorify an "organic" society based on the natural differences among men. In Popper's view Plato was a racist who longed for a stable, organic, tribal life, and who was so unfaithful to the undogmatic character of his teacher, Socrates, that he designed a political code that would prevent inquiry and dissent, and that Socrates obviously could not live with. R. H. S. Crossman has argued in a similar vein that Plato betrayed the liberal spirit of Socrates and wrote the most savage attack on democratic ideals that history can show.[2]

In assessing the contentions of Popper and Crossman, one should keep in mind several points. First of all, Plato does not contrast individuals and societies as he does contrast particulars and Forms. Indeed, he repeatedly compares an individual to a society, claiming that we are all a consortium of agencies. The theory of the Forms thus does not, by itself, dictate Plato's political views. It is his teleology that is of first importance. A human, not divine, purpose

1. Karl R. Popper, *The Open Society and its Enemies*, 2 vols. (London: Routledge and Kegan Paul, 1949), 1, chaps. 6, 7, and 8.

2. R. H. S. Crossman, "Plato and the Perfect State," in *Plato: Totalitarian or Democrat?*, T. L. Thorson (Englewood Cliffs, N.J.: Prentice Hall, 1963).

should rule the state. Second, the separable, supernatural reason of man is more comparable to a Form than it is to any visible entity. Individuals for Plato are not unreal—the Forms themselves are "single things"—and the opposition in his system is not between part and whole, individual and state—but between things seen and unseen—body and soul, particular and Form. Thus he does not regard the state as any more real than its citizens. Third, the "naturalism" of Plato that Popper and Crossman both write about has nothing to do with race or biological distinctions of any kind. There is in the *Republic* talk of a ruler's spreading the "noble lie" that men are by nature suited to various stations in life, but that talk is admittedly a lie designed to secure allegiance from people who are accustomed to think of organic nature as the hallmark of the just. For Plato it is the capacity of a man to know and the power of his soul to rule his body that should determine his social status; ethnic identity, race, and biology have nothing to do with the matter. Plato's loyalties are neither to organic nature nor to collectivities as such, but to the souls of men and to the true Nature—the *physis*—of the Forms to which the soul is akin and that it may know. The stringent political controls of his utopia are not, in his view, tyrannical. They are, indeed, designed to secure freedom for everything human in us. Unless helped by a political reformer, we can only stay enmeshed in the restrictive mud and seaweed of organic life. Fourth, the program of censorship and thought control that Plato outlines in the *Laws* is a simple consequence of the hypothesis he is entertaining—a hypothesis that is in full harmony with the doctrines he attributes to the supposedly "liberal" Socrates. In a society where administrators are unknowing imitators, virtue cannot be taught. Other devices, such as censorship and rote memorization, must be used. His doctrine is most certainly not a departure from Socratic contentions, for one of Socrates's most characteristic claims is that none of the major figures of Greek political life could teach virtue. All were unknowing imitators with a knack for ruling, but without a true art. Thus Plato's political philosophy clearly stems from a set of theories about man, not from atavistic and unreasoned attitudes. It is a political philosophy, too, that remains true to the precepts credited to Socrates in the very earliest of the dialogues.

If an objective reader were to agree with these assessments, and so conclude that Plato does not altogether deserve the harsh rebukes of his critics, he would nonetheless have to acknowledge that there are a lot of unattractive and fairly basic political precepts in the dialogues. He would, at any rate, have to demur at the efforts of some of Plato's recent defenders to turn him into a champion of modern, democratic ideals. Ronald Levison has argued thoughtfully against Plato's major critics, but he concludes his study with the dubious claim that a sympathetic reader could easily rid Plato's political recommendations of their more repugnant aspects and retain the rest as a guide for a democratic society. He holds, for example, that we can keep Plato's utopian ideal of the union of political power with reason, while rejecting the inconsistent and overzealous demands for class stratification, thought control, and censorship of the arts.[3] Plato's position, however, is one of extreme unity of doctrine. Given the hypothesis that two teleologies meet in us, one human the other divine, he concludes that the human reason should rule for the sake of both freedom and justice. Its rule, too, should be enforced by a stratification of classes. There is no other way its authority could be guaranteed, since there is an innate and pervasive force in our lives opposed to it. Without institutional support, it couldn't control the state. Likewise, given the hypothesis that the arts produce mental conflict by encouraging in us the rule of the

3. Ronald Levison, *In Defense of Plato* (Cambridge, Mass.: Harvard University Press, 1953), pp. 570-79.

wrong teleology, they need to be censored. Since, too, the unknowing cannot teach virtue, some form of extra-argumentative persuasion is mandatory in a state administered by those without knowledge. There is no way of detaching these repugnant conclusions from Plato's position without violating the thematic unity and conceptual coherence of his system. They are not, as Levison suggests, inconsistencies, disillusioned abandonments of principle, or lapses from insight to be weeded out of the dialogues. They are straightforward consequences of beliefs basic to his philosophy. Just as a sympathetic student of Plato cannot mute the *Republic*'s attack on art without misinterpreting it, so he cannot refashion that same dialogue's demands for political reform without distorting them.

For a similar reason an objective and fair-minded reader must be chary of accepting the claims of John Wild[4] and John H. Hallowell[5] that Plato is a prime source of the ideas on natural law that have been of such importance in the modern world in securing for individuals some protection from their governments. Wild and Hallowell emphasize Plato's commitment to a principle of "natural justice" that makes him critical, they feel, of autocratic rule and arbitrary law. In their view some things are simply right and other things are simply wrong for Plato, and thus all officials and all laws may be judged as just or unjust. The state remains accountable to a principle independent of it. Legislation and decree, being matters of convention, have to be sanctioned by nature before they can claim to be morally binding on those they affect. Wild argues that by virtue of this doctrine Plato deserves credit for being possibly one of the first, and certainly one of the most important, theorists

4. John Wild, "Plato as an Enemy of Democracy: A Rejoinder," in *Plato: Totalitarian or Democrat?*, ed. T. L. Thorson (Englewood Cliffs, N.J.: Prentice Hall, 1963).

5. John H. Hallowell, "Plato and the Moral Foundations of Democracy," in *Plato: Totalitarian or Democrat?*, ed. T. L. Thorson.

to stand firm against sophistic relativity in moral and legal matters and to set philosophical limits on the arbitrary use of power. For that reason he has a claim to the respect, even the gratitude, of all modern political liberals.

There is, possibly, some truth to the speculation that Plato's views have influenced modern conceptions of natural law; but if there is, it is surely owing to a mistaken reading of his position. Plato clearly uses "nature" in a normative sense, as Wild and Hallowell emphasize. As they also point out, he is, too, a moral realist. But these features of his thought do nothing whatsoever to establish his originality or to distinguish him from a fair number of the sophistic skeptics and totalitarians he attacks and from whom, Wild claims, he has helped to save us. Antiphon and Callicles, among others, used "nature" in a normative sense, holding in the manner of the moral realist that all self-interested modes of behavior are objectively and naturally right. Yet they are scarcely important contributors to progressive ideals in modern legal theory. In his realism and normative use of "nature" Plato has no more significance in the history of jurisprudence than some of the most nihilistic moral and political thinkers of antiquity.

Then, too, one must keep in mind that for Plato laws, as such, are always products of convention and imitation, of use only to imitators who never model their work on what is truly natural: the Forms. The philosopher-king and the tyrant are alike in ruling without law. Neither is a constitutional head of state. In the case of the philosopher there is no harm, only advantage, in the absence of constitutional restraints, for he has a capacity for knowledge and consequently can decide all important issues on a reasonable, case by case basis. He has no need for laws to help him determine what is best or right. Therefore, in a utopia there would be no law, natural or otherwise, to guide the ruler's decisions. In the case of an imitative order, law would exist, and it would be described by its makers as natural law (*Laws* 890 D). Their description, however, would be largely a forensic point, resting on the observation that everything in appearance is a matter of convention, or *nomos*, and that no invidious distinction can be drawn between the artificial and the natural in this world. Plato's point is that if people want to call the plant and animal kingdoms natural, they have no right to refuse that title to the imitative conventions of the state. If they do refuse, they are guilty of not understanding the artificiality of everything in life (*Laws* 892 B). Strictly speaking, then, there is no such thing as a natural law for Plato. Neither is any law a direct participant in what is natural: the *physis* of the Forms. Plato can be cited as a believer in the notion that some laws are natural only by miscasting his arguments and by ignoring his basic metaphysical stand.

The philosopher-reformer of the *Republic* would, to be sure, make use of a principle of "natural justice" that would make his utopia in some sense a natural city, but that principle amounts only to the simple doctrine that people with similar capacities should be given similar pursuits (*Republic* 456 B). It has nothing to do with any doctrine—traditionally associated with natural-law theory—of natural rights that would give a substantial moral content to Plato's precept. There is in the *Republic* and the *Laws*, for example, no recognition of an inalienable, natural right to life, liberty, property, or anything else. Defective children can be purged. Travel may be severely restricted, and the state does not recognize any right to pursue one's inclinations in such delicate matters as choice of ideology, mate, or profession. If natural law is the law that is violated when a natural right is violated, Plato has little claim to being a natural law theorist. As far as the utopian city's being natural is concerned, that point rests on the contention that its features would reflect more clearly than any other city's the Forms and the structure of the personality—a contention that is obviously dependent on Plato's psychological and metaphysical views turning out to be true. Like everything else in the world, however, the utopian city would be a product of art. Only entities capable of a spaceless and timeless existence are truly natural. The actual, functioning political precepts that Plato adopts thus stem from his highly contentious theories about man and the world. A rejection of those theories would invite a rejection of his precepts. The only way to retain anything very substantial from Plato's political doctrines is to be a Platonist.

It is enough, by way of coming to Plato's defense, to point out that his most violent critics have seriously misread him. It is excessive to try turning either him or Socrates into the political liberals they were not. Participants on both sides of the controversy are guilty of failing to see what his motives were and of allowing themselves to be misled by his claim that an ideal state would be a natural city. Popper thinks that claim makes Plato some kind of primitive racist with loyalties to organic, ethnic groupings. Wild thinks it makes him the intellectual predecessor of John Locke and other civil libertarians who find in nature a ground for limiting state action. It is a claim, however, that Plato simply makes in behalf of an urban culture that his sophistic opponents had indicated as unnatural. His substantive point is that everything in the cosmos is unnatural and that, therefore, we cannot possibly live in a state of nature with natural laws and natural institutions. We ought, he concludes, honor our own, human arts and seek to add to and aid the divine art we mistakenly call nature. In ordinary terms that conclusion amounts to a defense of all that is artificial in our lives and, if not to a full indictment, at least to a sharp critique of all that is natural. Plato's political interests are not to be understood as an early version of modern demands for ethnic and racial self determination. Neither are they to be understood as an early version of modern demands for middle-class autonomy. They are to be understood in terms of his desire to defend the form of life his civilization took. His loyalties are simply to the city-state.

Conclusion: The Unity of Plato's Position and Two Pleas on How To Read His Dialogues

Plato's loyalties to the city-state combine with his belief in the values of science and education to set a framework around his discussions of metaphysics, epistemology, psychology, aesthetics, and politics. One way to describe that framework—and in describing it to summarize the thesis of this book—is to say that Plato was fundamentally preoccupied in all his writing with the contrast between art and nature. That preoccupation is central to his defense of science and education and to his justification of an urban style of life. It is a preoccupation that ties together his basic ambitions and that gives a structural unity to his philosophical system.

Plato's interest in the contrast between art and nature took the form of trying to temper it. He tried in two ways. First, he argued that what is ordinarily thought of as nature is actually divine art. The difference between culture and nature is, then, really the difference between human *nomos* and divine *nomos*. Culture, he argued, is not something different in kind from nature; it is simply an addition to and an improvement on divine culture. On that difference rests Plato's teleological dualism—a dualism that is clearly part of an effort to replace the full contrast of art to nature with a tempering distinction. Plato, of course, did not deny that there is a nature. The whole world of sensory appearance may be art, but there still stands opposed to it a Natural, real realm occupied by what he called the Forms. Thus the contrast between art and nature reappears in his system as a distinction between appearance and reality. In describing that distinction he made a second effort to temper the contrast between the artificial and the natural. The art work of appearance aspires, he held, to the Natural condition of reality. *Nomos* represents *physis*, thereby partaking of its qualities. Thus appearance is not something utterly opposed to and in contradiction with reality. Rather, it is merely an incomplete and imperfect version of reality. On that distinction rests Plato's ontological dualism—a dualism that is also clearly part of an effort to replace the full contrast of art to nature with a tempering distinction.

Plato was interested in finding affinities between the artificial and the natural so as to relieve the skeptical tensions of his basic beliefs. He wanted to undermine the moral and cultural nihilism of those who found in the supposedly natural pursuit of self-interest the hallmark of justice. He wanted, however, to retain their central and traditional principle that what is just is what is natural. Thus he argued that the amoral way of life of savages and animals cannot be credited with a natural standing. Nature, so called, is really art. It is, too, art that, when compared to the art of man, is incomplete and botched. We have, then, good reason to avoid living in a state of "nature." We have equally good reason to avoid, if possible, living in a cultural order that merely imitates, without adding to and aiding, the plant and animal kingdoms. Plato also wanted to undermine the scientific nihilism of those who found in the supposedly natural state of rest the hallmark of intelligibility. He wanted, however, to retain their principle that only a motionless Nature—*physis*—is fully coherent. Thus he argued that motion, like art, is a product of soul, and that the moving realm of appearance has been made by its designers in such a way that it reflects, through its motions, certain features of a reality that only our minds can grasp. The art work of sensible appearance is an incomplete and imperfect version of an intelligible reality. It is, then, at least partially coherent, and we have good reason not to dismiss the whole of the testimony of our senses as utterly false. Plato's two related efforts to undermine the contrast of art to nature result in parallel theories of how culture is related to nature, so called, and how thought is related to sensation. Those theories unify Plato's position. They also fulfill his aims by serving to justify an inquiring, urban form of life that his basic convictions had called into doubt.

An interpretation of Plato along these lines is one that must make a cardinal plea for the reading of his work in the light of the sociological and historical factors surrounding it. Plato's philosophical system is, in essence, an exercise in cultural self-justification. He was the founder of what, in effect, was the world's first great university, and in that enterprise he obviously had to have had the support of his fellow Athenians. He was, too, the most eloquent defender of the urban form of life his civilization adopted. Yet he was a man of skeptical convictions who shared with many of the most thoughtful men of his day doubts about the utility of inquiry and the propriety of living out one's life in the conventional confines of the city-state. Surely it must seem to anyone a paradox that the man who probably did most to advance the cause of higher education in Greek antiquity and to justify its urban style of life was a man who believed that the world is unknowable and that our true home is in a purely Natural realm. Any sense of undue paradox will be weakened, however, by the observation that the tensions in Plato's work between skeptical conviction and philosophical aim are neither bizarre nor crankishly private. They are tensions that reflect the intellectual problems of his age. In trying to extricate himself from his skepticism, Plato was also trying to justify in terms of its own philosophical heritage an urban and scientifically oriented society that had developed doubts about some of its most distinctive values. Plato's dialogues are really the record of a man who is trying to harmonize the philosophical traditions of a society with its way of life. Their portrait of Socrates as a city-loving sage who yet reveres Nature is a portrait of the philosopher in whom that harmony has been achieved. Like some of his most distinguished predecessors, Socrates believed that only an unmoving Nature is knowable and that only a life lived in accord with Nature is just. Yet he firmly believed in the value of inquiry, arguing that although right opinion may be all that we can attain to in empirical matters, it is certainly not an illusory enterprise of no worth to reflect on the conditions of life. He firmly believed, too, in the essential rectitude of the city-state as man's proper, interim home. As described by Plato, he is the philosopher who has found in the traditions of philosophy the means of supporting, rather than undermining, the values of an urban society that has itself supported the intellectual efforts that philosophy represents.

To read Plato's dialogues as the record of an attempt to harmonize a society's way of life with its philosophical heritage is to have at least a partial explanation for what is, perhaps, their most puzzling aspect. Plato responded to the skeptical issues that bothered him in an odd, peculiar manner—a manner so odd and peculiar, indeed, that he was obliged to argue for paradox after paradox to support his case. It would have been best, it must surely seem to most, for him to have attacked directly the premises of the moral and scientific nihilists he opposed. Instead, he accepted their premises, then tried to avoid their conclusions. Why, one may well ask, didn't he simply deny that nature has anything to do with morality and justice? Why, too, didn't he deny that only the unmoving is intelligible? One answer is, of course, that these are not overly easy matters to deny. To call an action unnatural is even today a way of indicting it, and so there does seem to be some genuine, conceptual connection between the natural and the right. Likewise, the difficulties Plato faced in making sense of motion were severe enough that virtually every generation of mathematicians has been dissatisfied with the way its predecessors have dealt with them. Many a moralist and many a mathematician has given Antiphon and Zeno a fall only to win, in the judgments of history, no lasting victory. There is no reason, then, to think that Plato was not convinced that his opponents' central tenets were correct. Still, unlike almost everyone else who has been bothered by what bothered him, Plato made no serious effort to refute the troublesome notions that only what is natural is just and only what is unmoving is intelligible. A likely reason he acquiesced so readily to the premises of his opponents is that their views represented an important strand of philosophical tradition. Starting with Thales in the sixth century B.C., and then continuing throughout early Greek thought, anything identified as Nature is almost invariably treated as an object of reverence. It is, too, almost invariably the ultimate object of knowledge and of scientific inquiry, which explains, perhaps, the moving, sensible cosmos but without being a part of it. Even the atomists, who uncharacteristically equated Nature, or *physis*, with moving particles, were careful to claim that what is truly Natural—the atoms—is indestructible and at least qualitatively constant. Some of the power of the position maintained by Parmenides and Zeno thus stemmed from the point that it was not just illogical, but bordering on the blasphemous, to say of a religiously conceived and revered *physis* that it changed in any way. Plato's own stand is in remarkable harmony with a philosophical tradition that virtually defined Nature as an unchanging, intelligible substance. It would seem that he wanted to have the sanctions of that tradition for his own views. Thus he moved, not to refute, but to reconcile a set of moral and scientific presumptions on the standing of nature with the values of an intensely intellectual and urban way of life they had come to threaten. It simply was, so it would seem, his one great ambition to harmonize Greek philosophy with Greek culture.

Plato's efforts to effect the harmony he sought results in a dualistic system that is tightly knit and internally coherent but laden with paradox. To undermine the crucial contrasts of a degenerate art to a revered nature, he had to turn some ordinary linguistic oppositions into philosophical similarities. Procreation and portraiture are not the different processes we ordinarily assume they are. They are, Plato insists, essentially alike, for what we most readily call nature is really art. The movements of a temporal world are, too, but participants in an eternal realm; thus motion is not the opposite of rest, but a version of it. To support these key paradoxes Plato was obliged to argue for still other queer, unsettling tenets. He had, for example, to claim that most men understand neither the referents nor the meaning of what they say, that there is no true knowledge of anything empirical, and that in spite of appearances to the contrary, no ontologically significant distinction can be drawn between a three-dimensional physical object and a two-dimensional image.

Plato's paradoxes and his unsettling tenets present his reader with the difficult problem of deciding how to deal with what he wrote. What is one to make, for example, of the *Republic*'s claim that a carpenter merely represents the Couch that truly is when he builds a bed? How could, one is inclined to ask, anything that is timeless and spaceless be a couch? Two different kinds of answer are possible. One is that Plato didn't really mean what, at first blush, he seems to have meant, but something else. One can then try to supply that something else by appealing to one's own fund of notions on what a coherent and sensible doctrine would be. The history of Platonic scholarship is replete with efforts of this kind to "reinterpret" and to explain away the most puzzling aspects of Plato's text. A second kind of answer is that the dialogues should be taken at face value. A major aim of this book is to show how that can be done. It is an aim that has not been entirely fulfilled, for no effort has been made to render a full, definitive interpretation of Plato's work. I hope enough has been done, however, to be able to enter a persuasive plea for the reading of the dialogues in a literal vein.

In entering this plea I would caution my reader to keep in mind two points. One is that Plato will sometimes make use of a self-issued license to pronounce on what a literal reading of his text would come to. For example, the Form Couch is a literal couch in Plato's view, but he doesn't mean by *couch* what we think we mean when using that word in daily life. We are under the impression that couches are pieces of furniture we can sit on. For Plato, however, what we call couches are only apparent couches. The Couch that truly is a couch is something purely intelligible. Thus, although Plato means what he says, his doctrines should be read by the light of his theory of meaning and language. A second, related point is that even when Plato has no interest in using the license his philosophy of language gives him to assign words a special meaning, his arguments occur in the context of an unusual cosmology that often affects, not the sense, but the truth value of what he writes. For example, pictures of couches would seem to be literal imitations of couches in Plato's view, but he wants to call them imitations only because they represent what he considers to be other pictures. Here he seems to mean by *imitation* what everyone else means, but the truth of what he writes is dependent on the truth of his philosophical themes on the status of appearance. A literal reading of Plato should, then, be attempted only from his, not from one's own, point of view. Otherwise the aura of paradox that pervades his dialogues will not be dispelled.

I think that there are several good reasons why, with due caution, one should read Plato in a literal vein. Taking his doctrines at face value will, first of all, pay him the important courtesy any reader owes a great writer of leaving what he says intact and of acknowledging that he probably had an intelligent reason for putting matters the way he did. Interpretations that explain away Plato's most puzzling claims must, after all, either alter or dismiss at least a portion of his text; and although most interpretations of this kind have had as their directing motive the defense of his intelligence they must, in the end, charge him with naiveté, prejudice, ignorance, or confusion. Many a sympathetic "reinterpretation" of Plato has, indeed, ended up voicing the wish that he had been a little more astute, fair, clear headed, or knowledgeable. The easiest and safest way to do justice to both Plato and his work is simply to refrain from tampering with what he wrote.

Second, if one surrenders to the logic of the metaphors Plato uses, and if one tries to fit together his tenets without bending or breaking them, the internal coherence of his position will emerge. It will emerge, of course, only because one has exercised a certain willing suspension of common sense; and that may strike some as an irresponsible way to read a text; but it is, I think the only way to read Plato. His position is inherently paradoxical if judged in terms of ordinary conviction. The structure of his system cannot be left intact, or even perceived, if one insists on reading him as an author with whom most everyone might well agree. The best way to understand him—like everyone else—is to assume that he means what he says. That assumption may, at times, be difficult to make; nonetheless, it should be tried.

A third reason for reading Plato in a literal vein is that it helps one avoid falling back on dubious stands that amount, in effect, to abandonments of any effort to understand his texts. A significant number of Plato's commentators have given up trying to explain his views on various topics, especially the arts, on the ground that only psychology and psychoanalysis can answer the question of why he argued in the queer, unsettling manner he did. No matter what one's opinion of the explanatory value of psychoanalysis might be, it must surely be admitted that it will be a long time, indeed, before Plato is understood if we have to wait for a definitive analysis of his unknown mental disorders. A similar observation must hold for those who have felt that we have to wait upon the judgments of the philologist and the grammarian before we can grasp what Plato really had in mind. Postponements of the effort to understand are likely to be permanent and should, for that reason, be discouraged. Since postponements often rest on the assumption that there is a difference between the unknown reality and the known appearance of an author's intent, it is merely prudent strategy to proceed as if a text means what it says.

A fourth, and my last, reason for urging that Plato's dialogues be taken at face value is that artificial postulates of vacillation and evolution in his basic doctrines are more difficult to make if it is assumed that he really did mean just what he said. Rather than deny outright that Plato argued for some of the unsettling doctrines he seems to have argued for, many of his commentators have held that he changed his mind as he grew older. It must be admitted, of course, that Plato was capable of a change of mind. It must be admitted, too, that he probably did alter some of his views as he thought them over. Who hasn't? Still, more vacillation and evolution have been attributed to Plato than the evidence of his texts warrants. Some commentators have held that he wisely gave up his queer, confused theory of the Forms when reaching his full conceptual powers in late maturity. In contrast, others have held that the *Laws* represents an old man's disillusioned change of heart and an unfortunate turning away from the hopeful political idealism of the *Republic*. There is only the most dubious evidence that these claims are true. The *Timaeus*, for example, would appear to be a fairly late dialogue, and there the Forms are recognized. The kind of imitative state the *Laws* describes is also clearly allowed for, even foreshadowed, in the political classifications recognized in earlier dialogues, such as the *Sophist*, the *Republic*, and the *Meno*. Plato's thought is very systematic. Attributing fundamental changes of mind to him is often motivated more by a desire to rescue him from an unsettling text than it is by any need to reconcile obviously incompatible stands. It is too easy, and too myopic, to attribute what one does not like about him either to his youth or his old age, whichever seems more convenient, and to link what one does like to either a mature wisdom or a youthful vigor, whichever meets with one's views on the merits of age. There is, in essence, only one Plato, and he should not be divided into two or more by assuming that although he may have meant what he said, he only meant it for a time in an aberrant moment, perhaps, or during a clouded stage of life.

Anyone who is even partially persuaded by my pleas on how Plato's work should be read may ask the question of why it should be read at all. If his dialogues reflect the intellectual problems of his age, and if they resolve those problems in an odd, unsettling way, then what contemporary relevance or appeal might they have? All the standard answers that justify the study of intellectual history might, of course, be given here, but I will end with a single observation for which I have no explanation. The disquieting aspects of Plato's stands can be read, I have urged, as the result of his efforts to reconcile a philosophical heritage with a style of life. His acute sensitivity to the peculiar intellectual, historical, and cultural issues of a day long past may make it seem that his appeal must be limited. Yet, he has been an enormously influential writer who has struck a responsive chord in the minds of a very large number of readers. Rather than see anything paradoxical about these facts, I think they should be seen as connected. It is precisely the writer whose troubled work is shaped by the fundamental tensions of his time and his place who often proves to be of perennial interest. Why that should be true, I am not sure, although guesses are easy to make. What is important is to recognize that it is true. If I have any readers who doubt it, I leave them with the argument of this book to confute and the appeal of Plato to account for in some other way.

Modern Authors and Works Cited

Adam, James. *The Republic of Plato*. Cambridge: Cambridge University Press, 1902; rpt. 1965.

Allen, R. E. "Participation and Predication in Plato's Middle Dialogues." In *Studies in Plato's Metaphysics*, edited by R. E. Allen. London: Routledge and Kegan Paul, 1965.

Beardsley, M. C. *Aesthetics from Classical Greece to the Present*. New York: Macmillan, 1966.

Bosanquet, B. *A History of Aesthetic*. New York: Meridian Books, 1957.

Callahan, J. F. *Four Views of Time in Ancient Philosophy*. Cambridge, Mass.: Harvard University Press, 1948.

Cherniss, H. F. "The Relation of the *Timaeus* to Plato's Later Dialogues." In *Studies in Plato's Metaphysics*, edited by R. E. Allen. London: Routledge and Kegan Paul, 1965.

Collingwood, R. G. "Plato's Philosophy of Art." *Mind* 34: 154-72.

Coomaraswamy, Ananda K. "Vedic Exemplarism." *Harvard Journal of Asiatic Studies* 1: 44-64, 281.

Copleston, F. *A History of Philosophy*. Garden City, N.Y.: Doubleday and Company, 1962.

Cornford, F. M. *Plato's Cosmology*. New York: Liberal Arts Press, 1957.

Crombie, I. M. *An Examination of Plato's Doctrines*. London: Routledge and Kegan Paul, 1963.

Crossman, R. H. S. "Plato and the Perfect State." In *Plato: Totalitarian or Democrat?*, edited by T. L. Thorson. Englewood Cliffs, N.J.: Prentice Hall, 1963.

Eliade, Mircea. *Cosmos and History: The Myth of the Eternal Return*. New York: Pantheon Books, 1954.

Else, G. F. "Imitation in the Fifth Century." *Classical Philology* 53: 73-90.

Freud, Sigmund. *Beyond the Pleasure Principle*. New York: Bantam Books, 1959.

Friedlander, Paul. *Plato: An Introduction*. New York: Harper and Row, 1964.

Geach, P. T. "The Third Man Again." In *Studies in Plato's Metaphysics*, edited by R. E. Allen. London: Routledge and Kegan Paul, 1965.

Gilbert, K. and Kuhn, H. *A History of Esthetics*. New York: Macmillan, 1939.

Greene, W. C. "Plato's View of Poetry." *Harvard Studies in Classical Philology 29: 1-75.*

Grube, G. M. A. *Plato's Thought*. Boston: Beacon Press, 1958.

Guthrie, W. K. C. *A History of Greek Philosophy*. Cambridge: Cambridge University Press, 1962.

Hack, R. K. "The Doctrine of Literary Forms." *Harvard Studies in Classical Philology 27: 1-66.*

Hallowell, John H. "*Plato and the Moral Foundations of Democracy.*" In *Plato: Totalitarian or Democrat?*, edited by T. L. Thorson. Englewood Cliffs, N.J.: Prentice Hall, 1963.

Havelock, E. A. *Preface to Plato*. Cambridge, Mass.: Harvard University Press, 1963.

Koller, Herman. *Die Mimesis in der Antike*. Bern: Francke, 1954.

Levison, R. *In Defense of Plato*. Cambridge, Mass.: Harvard University Press, 1953.

Lodge, R. C. *Plato's Theory of Art*. London: Routledge and Kegan Paul, 1953.

Lovejoy, Arthur O. *The Great Chain of Being*. Cambridge, Mass.: Harvard University Press, 1936.

McKeon, R. "Literary Criticism and the Concept of Imitation in Antiquity." *Modern Philology* 34: 1-35.

Moravscik, J. M. E. "The 'Third Man' Argument and Plato's Theory of Forms." *Phronesis* 8: 50-62.

Morrow, Glen R. "Necessity and Persuasion in Plato's *Timaeus*." In *Studies in Plato's Metaphysics*, edited by R. E. Allen. London: Routledge and Kegan Paul, 1965.

Murphy, Neville R. *The Interpretation of Plato's Republic*. London: Oxford University Press, 1951.

Peck, A. L. "Plato versus Parmenides." *Philosophical Review* 71: 159-84.

Peterson, S. "A Reasonable Self-Predication Premise for the Third Man Argument." *Philosophical Review* 82: 451-70.

Popper, Karl. *The Open Society and its Enemies*. London: Routledge and Kegan Paul, 1949.

Rankin, K. W. "The Duplicity of Plato's Third Man." *Mind* 78: 178-97.

Runciman, W. G. "Plato's Parmenides." In *Studies in Plato's Metaphysics*, edited by R. E. Allen. London: Routledge and Kegan Paul, 1965.

Ryle, G. *Plato's Progress*. Cambridge: Cambridge University Press, 1966.

Shiner, R. A. "Self-Predication and the 'Third Man' Argument." *Journal of the History of Philosophy* 8: 371-86.

Tate, Jonathan. "'Imitation' in Plato's Republic." *Classical Quarterly* 22: 16-23.

———. "Plato and 'Imitation.'" *Classical Quarterly* 26: 161-69.

Taylor, A. E. *A Commentary on Plato's Timaeus*. London: Oxford University Press, 1928.

Verdenius, W. J. *Mimesis: Plato's Doctrine of Artistic Imitation and its Meaning to Us*. Leiden: Brill, 1962.

Vlastos, G. "Postscript to the Third Man: A Reply to Mr. Geach." In *Studies in Plato's Metaphysics*, edited by R. E. Allen. London: Routledge and Kegan Paul, 1965.

———. "The Unity of the Virtues in the *Protagoras*." *Review of Metaphysics* 25: 415-58.

———. "The Disorderly Motion in the *Timaeus*." In *Studies in Plato's Metaphysics*, edited by R. E. Allen. London: Routledge and Kegan Paul, 1965.

Warry, J. C. *Greek Aesthetic Theory*. New York: Barnes and Noble, 1962.

Wild, John. "Plato as an Enemy of Democracy: A Rejoinder." In *Plato: Totalitarian or Democrat?*, edited by T. L. Thorson. Englewood Cliffs, N.J.: Prentice Hall, 1963.

Index

DATE DUE